CRUMP

Published by Advita LLC
P.O. Box 30246
Honolulu, HI 96820
advitallc@gmail.com

First Edition softcover 2012

ISBN-13: 978-0-9847995-2-7

Design: Toelke Associates www.toelkeassociates.com

Printed in the USA

10 9 8 7 6 5 4 3 2 1

The Nebraska high-school football coach
who was not what we wanted,
but just what we needed

CRUMP

by Bob Thomas

Advita LLC
Honolulu, Hawaii

Dedication

To the two most important coaches in my life,
in appreciation of the love they showered upon me:

My mother, Lois, who guided and supported me
in all ways a parent could, and

My wife and life partner, Avis,
who inspires me daily.

Acknowledgments

Many people contributed their memories and recollections, and I am indebted to all. They include Bruce Allen, Duane Andre, Marv Binegar, Byron Boslau, Trisha Bystrom Trowbridge, Herb Burch, Marilyn Ferguson Thyng, Sandy Fritz Booker, Bobby Gray, Millie Grosh, Lowell Harvey, Jim Huffman, Harold Kay, Stephen Kay, Alan Kehr, Mike Kirkman, Jim Kubicek, Bruce Kuhlmann, David Lile, Jim McFarland, Mary McMurtry States, Don Milroy, Olinda Odean Boslau, Butch Rasmussen, Robert Romeiser, Gary Scheet, Gary Sexson, Galen Skinner, Debra Smith, Jim States, Bill Stephenson, Lynn Stockall, Don Titus, Pete Tatman, Rodger Tuenge, Rodney Tuenge, Larry Wachholtz, Milan Wall, Bill Weekly, Anne Welch Weddell, Allan Whitesel, Judy Wilkinson Baker, and Tom Wisdom.

I also appreciate others who read my work and offered their opinions, including May Ann Beamer, Iris Chung, John Gill, Gary Hardin, Jim Kellenberger, Denny Lewis, Bob McPhee, John Nystrom, and Dick Robinson.

I offer a special thanks to Coach Redding, Clark Redding, Dave Redding, and the extended Redding family, and to those who admirably served North Platte athletics over the years: Del Bailar, York Hinman, Clarence Kubicek, and Jerry Lee.

I commend the many students, teachers, and professionals who dedicated countless hours creating the school annuals, newspaper articles, and photos that comprised much of my research.

Ever since I wrote my first paragraph years ago, I've received invaluable assistance from:

Avis, who prodded me to start this project and then steadfastly held the standard high,

Larry Dietz, who helped me get started,

Matthew Kumin, who early on provided useful insights,

Amy Holden Jones, whose proven stature in the entertainment industry belied her willingness to do an editing deep-dive to help a friend and literary novice,

Gail Honda, my wonderful Hawaii editor whose expertise and professionalism were invaluable, and

The talented book editor Laurie Rosin, who helped put the ball over the goal line.

Finally, I thank those who supported me and inspired me during the writing of this book:

Wayne and Marti Huizenga, who are the grandest people to grace this earth,

The exceptional Steinlauf family, most notably Peter and Avi, who along with friends Jeremy, Charlie, Ken, Seth, Matt, Mike, and others, created a wonderful Internet company, and

My extended family and friends in Hawaii and the mainland.

Contents

Preface

The individuals and their accomplishments in this narrative are real. The athletic events are as accurate as memories and research can make them.

All the same, it happened decades ago. The following areas thus require additional explanation:

Conversations

Obviously, I cannot recall exact conversations from fifty years ago. Often I took conversations that occurred at different times or during my research and condensed them into situations that fit within the story timeline. For example, the dialogue attributed to Coach Redding is his, but a substantial portion was obtained later during my research.

Secondary stories

Nearly all happened as depicted, but in the interest of overall story development, there were instances where I took liberties with timelines and substituted people already known to the reader.

Photos

One final caveat is needed to address the variable quality of the photos. No one archived the photographs of those years—not the school, the newspaper, nor the photography studios. The pictures depicted throughout the story are taken from a combination of original photos kept as part of personal collections, newspaper articles pulled out of scrapbooks, and the school's annual yearbooks.

Introduction

Have you ever had someone in your life so positively affect you that today you could call that person your "mentor"? Have you ever been part of a group that underwent a performance transformation that astounded you? Have you ever had a dream or aspiration you felt so passionate about that you wrote it down as a declaration? And yes, have you ever suffered a public or private defeat and humiliation that shook you to your core?

● ● ●

Once forty years passed since my graduating from high school and I became conscious of our eventual fiftieth anniversary, I suddenly felt an increasing obligation to tell the story that follows. I'm not one to get mentally or emotionally stuck in any time period, but something compelling about this teenage experience called out to be memorialized.

On the surface, the only people affected were a group of boys, but that simplification is misleading. What transpired back then involved many others and had a lasting effect on all.

It would also be false to assume the remarkable achievement required an extraordinary set of youngsters. I was one of them, and I can assure you we were mostly unremarkable individually, though collectively capable.

What was unique regarding our potential in the aggregate? What was required for us to be inspired or even inspirable? What ultimately identified and assembled all of the pieces of the puzzle for us?

The answer to those questions came to our town in our junior year in the official position of a high-school football coach. The best way to depict his persuasive abilities is to describe him as the most forceful of the many tornadoes that regularly veered through the river valley where we lived.

We boys were adept at resisting the authority of coaches. We had been doing it for years across many sports. What was it about this coach that swept away our shields if not the powerful winds of his relentless nature?

While this book was written to commemorate our relationships with each other and with Coach Redding these many years ago, the road to our youthful awakening had many twists and turns.

To start with, as fifteen-year-olds, our entire focus was on a different coach and sport.

Bob Thomas, 2012

1

The Pledge

Our Pledge to Mr. Jim Smith
NPHS Varsity Basketball Coach

The undersigned,
Proud members of the 1959–60 freshman basketball team,
Undefeated in competition for the past two seasons,
Hereby declare ourselves
Nebraska State Basketball Champions
By the time we graduate from North Platte High School!

"State by '63!"

As our thirteen-member junior-high basketball team gathered after school in late spring, 1960, someone yelled out to me, "Bob, what made you think of this pledge-thing, anyway?"

"I can't take credit for it," I answered. "Two years ago, I read a book about a basketball team just like ours. After they went undefeated in junior high, they made a vow to become state champs."

"What happened?" he asked. "Did they give it to their high-school coach, too?"

"Yes, and he was so impressed and excited, he signed up with them and became a part of the commitment."

1

"Forget that," someone else chimed in. "Did they win the championship?"

"Yes. That's why when we completed the same perfect record these last two years, I decided it must have been Fate that had me read that book. That's when I thought we should sign our own pledge."

"I agree!"

"Let's do it."

"We're good enough."

"Can you read it to us one more time?"

I finally broke through the chatter and recited the document my mother had typed for me.

Afterward, I heard Larry Wachholtz's voice amid the approving murmurs. "I'm all for this as long as we take it seriously. This is a stupid thing to do if we don't mean it, but if we are committed, I'm in." When our best player and team leader spoke, everybody quieted down to reflect.

After a brief lull, the raucous atmosphere kicked in again. Our verbal affirmations were the same as a pact among boys around a campfire, our passion blending like blood droplets from knife cuts to our fingers.

"Yes!"

"We can do it!"

"We're definitely good enough!"

"I love it!"

"I'm in, too."

As we signed our team's Pledge, we cheered. I felt a palpable air of certainty and purpose springing from our youthful fervor. I could tell everyone was inspired by our intent, yet humbled by the personal commitment, obligation, and power flowing from our proud John Hancocks.

Slapping each other on our backs with congratulations, most of us self-assumed future state champs drifted out of the locker room, not knowing where to go without any sports practice scheduled.

Not me. I knew where to go.

Fulfilling the group's wishes, I walked next door to the senior-high building to hand deliver our declaration to Coach Smith. I was eager to set in motion a future I believed we had just created and documented for the ages.

As I walked along, I looked at the scrawled signatures next to our names. Mom had attached the list of players to our team photo and had recorded our names in the order we were seated.

Along the top were Allan Whitesel, Bob Romeiser, Bob Reuter, and Mike Kirkman. In the middle were Larry, seated next to Coach Bailar, then Lloyd Morris, Jim Huffman, Jim Meyer, and student manager Steve Van Cleave. On the bottom were Lowell Harvey, Jack Edwards, me, Darrel Gale, and David Lile. I had played countless hours with most of them in both organized and neighborhood sports in all kinds of weather over the years.

I had a sudden thought. I wondered if our names would be engraved on our state championship trophy.

The thirteen signers of the Pledge

After asking for directions, I finally arrived at Coach Smith's office. I knocked on his partially open door. He welcomed me in, pausing in his conversation with another teacher.

He accepted our document and glanced at it. "Thanks, Bob." He set it on his desk and returned to his conversation.

I was dumbstruck. It never dawned on me that Coach Smith wouldn't be as inspired by us as we were by ourselves. In the book I had read, the varsity coach had enthusiastically joined with his young players to chase their destiny. Our coach couldn't be bothered.

I was embarrassed.

Backing out of his office, I decided to keep his rebuff to myself. For one thing, I didn't want to look ridiculous in my friends' eyes. Besides, we hadn't needed him to go undefeated for two years in a row. We hadn't needed him to draft up the Pledge. We hadn't needed him to come together as a team and make an avowal regarding our future.

"State by '63!" was ours and ours alone.

We wouldn't need his participation in our proclamation to make it work. I would pretend he was in with us, and no one would be the wiser. He really had nothing at all to do with our predetermined fate.

No, even I had to admit to myself that wasn't exactly the case. How would we go about doing this sort of thing without our coach on board? We probably did need him after all.

I then worried whether we somehow caused his lack of interest. Did he think we were trying to place ourselves above him in importance? Did he have his own plan or timetable we stepped on? Did he . . .?

Ahhh, crap.

In a matter of moments, my feelings had changed from embarrassment to concern, and then to anger.

They settled on retribution. We'll show him!

2

Dull Thud

Coach Smith blew his whistle to get our attention over the sounds of bouncing basketballs and sneakers squeaking on the hardwood floor. He motioned for all of us eager athletes who had been trying out for his varsity basketball team to congregate on the bleachers. Seated where the band assembled during games, we filled as many rows high as they did.

I knew a lot of boys would be disappointed. I hoped I wasn't one of them.

As we settled in, he blew his whistle again for us to quiet down. He took off his glasses, cleaned them, and then began, "My choices today were not easy. These have been the most competitive tryouts in my time here as head coach. But I've made my decision for the 1960–'61 Bulldogs. For the first time, my selection is evenly divided among the three classes.

"First, I'll announce the seniors. Bob Carpenter, Terry Discoe, Gary Kosbau, and Denny Christianson, please step down and join me on the court. I want you to know I expect a great deal of leadership from you this year.

"Next, the juniors who made the team are Jim States, Bill Stephenson, Gene Jones, and Roy Wagner. Please come down and stand behind the seniors.

"Finally, after much consideration, I've added four sophomores to the varsity. They are Larry Wachholtz, Darrel Gale, Jim Huffman, and Bob Thomas. You four will also play JV ball along with the non-starting juniors. Please stand behind the juniors."

Larry, my closest friend on the team, gave voice to my excitement. "Way to go, Bob!" he said as we shook hands and gathered behind the others. I couldn't have been more proud.

Four of us from our freshman team had made the varsity. Maybe our Pledge had carried some weight with Coach Smith, after all.

Coach Smith then announced the junior varsity team, which he said he would also coach. Most of the rest of our former freshman team were on the JV squad, which made me happy. We would be spending a lot of time together at games and combined practices.

My plan had come together. I was ready to get the season going, the next step to claiming our destiny.

1960–1961 varsity basketball team, *from top to bottom and left to right:* Bob Carpenter; Bob Thomas and Bill Stephenson; Jim Huffman, Terry Discoe, and Jim States; Gary Kosbau, Gene Jones, Denny Christianson, and Roy Wagner; Coach Ray Fox, Manager Jerry Phillips, Larry Wachholtz ("wah-holtz"), Darrel Gale, and Coach Jim Smith

• • •

A few months earlier, my transition from junior to senior high had not felt as full of promise.

The classic architecture senior-high building was located only a few steps from our familiar two-story modern junior high, but it might as well have been in a different universe.

Everything was different and intimidating. Cocky upperclassmen went out of their way in the hallways to bump into us three hundred-plus sophomores and then growl at us to move aside for them. Between classes, the wide, three-story stairwells were like a stampede of cattle—noisy and chaotic.

I was having difficulty adjusting in more ways than one. After years of playing every sport I could, I had decided not to go out for football as a sophomore. I wanted to use that time to prepare to pursue our basketball dream. Besides, the varsity football team was as terrible as our junior-high football team had been. We had only won two games

North Platte Public High School

in each of our two years, and that was what the varsity had averaged for years.

Even so, it was a tough decision. I had never enjoyed playing football, but I found that I easily got caught up in varsity game-day excitement.

In junior high, our games had been like another class. They weren't anything the whole school participated in.

In senior high, it was way, way different. Game day was a big deal. Over two hundred Pep Club girls milled throughout the hallways, each member decked out in her white sweater with a Bulldog emblem on the front. Lettermen's Club members were everywhere as well, each one proudly wearing a colorful letter sweater or jacket.

Uniforms, supportive students and teachers, numerous banners, a thunderous band, and enthusiastic cheerleaders and Pep Club

Left: Representative letter jackets and sweaters worn during 1960–1961 school year; *Below:* 1960–1961 Pep Club members in uniform

members all combined to ratchet up the excitement meter.

But what really got me psyched was the "whisper day" tradition. Everyone—students and teachers alike—spoke in whispers throughout the hallways and stairwells the day of a game. This collective verbal restraint was purportedly to save our voices for the late-afternoon pep rally in the auditorium, where the cheerleaders and Pep Band got the crowd hopping. But the surprising result was that the stark contrast of the school's quietness to the usual uproar powerfully amped everyone's anticipation for the game.

Even as a non-participant, my blood flowed hot and fast. I could only imagine how I would feel once I played on a varsity team. I was envious of my five classmates who had made the varsity football squad. Larry, Pete Tatman, Allan Whitesel, Mike Kirkman, and Marv Binegar all had an elevated status in school. I hoped my time in the sun would come when basketball rolled around.

Larry, to no one's surprise, was the only sophomore to make the starting team. Always the top athlete in our class, he had regularly surpassed everyone's expectations in every sport since grade school.

For the team, though, results throughout the season continued to be disappointing. The town had long and well supported the boys, but as the losses piled up again, rumblings had begun forming about the need to replace the current coach, Bob Easter, himself a former North Platte athlete.

At the same time, I was having fun pursuing my basketball dreams. Two classmates—Darrel Gale and Jim Huffman—and I had persuaded the junior-high janitor to let us use the gym every night after school for our makeshift basketball practices. The junior-high gymnasium was used by the varsity for workouts and games, so we felt fortunate to have our off-season practice time in the same environment.

Darrel was both competitor and partner to Larry, as they played as a second-base/shortstop duo in baseball and as guards in basketball. At 5' 7", Darrel was shorter than Larry, but he was a jumping jack who could dunk the ball.

Every bit Larry's equal in many ways, Darrel, however, always played in Larry's shadow. That subordination ate at him, even as Larry was oblivious to the perception. Our teams always benefited, however, due to his constant effort to be better than Larry.

On the other hand, nothing bothered the lanky, mild-mannered Jim Huffman. He played the forward position and possessed an enviable soft-shooting touch, which made him a formidable offensive threat.

Our off-season workouts attracted several participants, the best of whom was junior Jim States. He was a lefty and played forward like no one I had ever seen. If I had ever thought before we were destined to capture a state championship, I now considered it a lock.

No uppity-upperclassman attitude emanated from Jim—just pure hustle and a desire to make everyone's game better. I knew he would make an ideal teammate.

Jim had broken his left wrist in football his sophomore year and so wasn't able to play basketball, either. He still wasn't cleared to play football as a junior, so basketball became his focus during the off-season.

We told him about our "State by '63!" pledge, and he jumped aboard. In private, I described my disappointing visit to Coach Smith's office. When Jim heard about Coach's non-reaction, he admitted he had his own concerns about Coach Smith.

Coach Smith had made Jim a student manager while he was injured, to keep him involved with the team. Being privy to the coach's confidential discussions gave Jim insights not normally available to a player. He wouldn't divulge any juicy stuff, but he warned me not to get too excited about playing on the varsity, being that I was only a sophomore.

He explained, "Coach Smith will pick his team, dole out playing time, and grant privileges such as bus seating according to class rank. In his view, experience is everything, so the seniors will get every consideration. He will be afraid to field a lineup without a lot of seniors in it."

I ignored his counsel, however. My only foray into thinking ahead was being eager to have Larry join us after football season, along with Jim States's buddy, Bill Stephenson. Jim had convinced us Bill, a junior end on the football team, would also be a huge addition to our unof-ficially expanded Pledge membership.

My sophomore year, which had started in confusion and unfamil-iarity, was working out even better than hoped for. And then on the day Coach Smith announced his varsity-team selectees, it was obvious to me Destiny was beckoning us. It seemed my decision to quit foot-ball had been validated.

But Jim's prediction was soon proven to be correct. All sea-son long, Coach Smith held us underclassmen back from playing together in a game. We logged a fair amount of game time individu-ally, but rarely were we able to perform to our strength and what we felt was the team's greatest potential by playing as a unit.

Throughout the season, however, Coach Smith kept up his tradi-tion of Wednesday night full-court, game-clock scrimmages between a senior-laden fivesome and us underclassmen challengers. And week after week, we racked up victory after victory. How could he not see what we saw and were proving—that somehow our combination of personalities, enthusiasm, and support for one another trumped any other advantages held by the more experienced seniors.

The seniors hated it as their weekly loss deficit grew while the season progressed. Wednesday nights felt like they became more of a battle than the weekend games against other schools.

As the varsity regular season wore on, we underclassmen took our pleasures from the practice sessions. We had no egos, possessed lots of hustle, and enjoyed total familiarity with one another from years of playing together in organized and neighborhood sports.

As for the games, we endured them as we sat together on the bench.

By the time the last weekend series of the regular season arrived, our Wednesday night scrimmages stood 8–0 in our underclassmen's favor, while our varsity's game record was only 8–7.

Then, when we underclassmen least expected it, we got a pleasant surprise. Our final Friday night regular-season game was in McCook. They fielded a tough team we knew could easily add to our loss col-umn, especially on their home court. We had barely beaten them at home earlier in the year when, with no time left, Darrel sank two free throws to win the game by one point.

After our pregame warm-ups, Coach Smith called the team together for final instructions.

"I want the following players to take off their warm-ups. States, Stephenson, Wachholtz, Gale, and Thomas, you will be starting tonight."

I was shocked because three of us had started and played much of the preceding JV game, which we won handily. My ears were ringing so loudly from the blood rushing into my head, I almost missed the rest of what he had to say.

"Let's see what you've got in a real game. Go out there and get them!"

At the end of the first quarter at McCook, we were on top 16–7. We continued to swamp them in the second quarter. When Coach Smith put the angry and embarrassed seniors back in the game, the five of us underclassmen sat together on the bench silently knocking knees and shoulders back and forth in self-congratulation.

We had shown Coach Smith. We had shown the seniors. We had shown everybody.

We finally had the momentum to go into the district tournament on our way to state. We figured we knew how our road to the state championship was going to play out.

Destiny instead thumbed her nose at us.

Saturday night, back in North Platte for the final home game and also two weeks later for the first game of the district playoffs to determine the state tournament teams, Coach Smith reverted to form and had us underclassmen ride the bench.

Two losses later, our season was kaput.

For me, it seemed much more than two more unnecessary defeats. Our first season in quest of our ultimate goal was over. It had ended with a dull thud.

For us underclassmen, our disappointment was mollified only by our persistent belief in ourselves. We also held a firm conviction that next year, Coach Smith would have no excuse not to play the five of us, along with classmate Jim Huffman, in some combination as his starting five.

Plus, strangely enough, given his starting-lineup blind spot, we liked Smith as a coach. As a former star player at Kansas State, he knew his stuff and had imported their style of play to our school. His approach of having a quick transition from defense to a thundering fast break on offense fit our group's mindset perfectly.

I could hardly wait for my junior year to roll around so we could get going.

In the back of my mind, though, I knew the following year would have to be the year for it to happen. That would be our last season with Jim States and Bill Stephenson. Those two players had become invaluable and irreplaceable components of our "State by '63!" dream.

If we didn't pull it off in our junior year, I feared our pledge would be on shaky ground.

3

Eye Patch

Mid-June, 1961

Our sophomore year had ended, and I was bored hanging out at home. It was the annual brief transition between school and my summer job at the Hanna Cattle Ranch, located ninety miles north of North Platte in the heart of the Nebraska Sandhills.

I was feeling sorry for myself because I had to leave North Platte and my baseball teammates again. My friends could look forward to a full summer of baseball and going to Lake Maloney for swimming and socializing.

I decided to hop on my bicycle and find a game—any game—with my buddies. The next day, most people would be tied up with family and church activities, so I thought this might be my last chance for a while to play sports with my friends.

I jumped on my bike. It felt good to be out riding around. The exercise was calming the drama in my mind, as I had been stewing about the varsity-basketball coaching situation. Coach Smith had resigned, having accepted a similar position in another state. I could hardly think straight.

His replacement, hired quickly, was Joe Folsom, who had coached varsity basketball in nearby Ogallala. Under Folsom, their Class B school owned several years of winning records and had always played us tough.

We disappointed veterans decided that wasn't good enough for us, however. Ogallala was a much smaller school, and we translated that into meaning Coach Folsom was not worthy of our team.

The varsity-football program had its own issue. The school board had fired Coach Easter. Given the team's abysmal record over several seasons, that action had long been anticipated but no replacement had yet been announced. The football post didn't matter much to me, though, since I had quit playing football.

My enjoyment of touring all of the familiar neighborhoods while looking for a game, turned to frustration. Where was everybody? Was I going to have to have to go home and sit around by myself on my last weekend in town?

Wait a minute! I spoke out loud to myself, startled by what I saw. What were all those guys doing on the varsity-football field? It was off-limits and always locked up. How'd they get in there?

Pedaling my bicycle around the south end of the field, I circled until I was between it and the back of the high school. Then I saw how they had gained entrance to the forbidden grounds. Someone on the maintenance crew must have left the gate unlocked.

By the open entrance was a tangle of bicycles. Larry's blue-and-white pickup truck with his lawnmowers in the bed was also there. I laid my bike down on the ground amid the others.

As I slid through the gate, I glanced at the guys playing shirts and skins touch football, and déjà vu washed over me.

Two years earlier on the Hanna ranch, riding my horse to check fences in distant pastures, I had come upon a group of young colts. They had not seen or smelled my horse or me, so I was able to sit in the saddle without my presence affecting what they were doing.

I watched as they slowly collected one-by-one into small groups and then suddenly scattered, darting in all directions. They seemed to revel in their newfound physical capabilities. As they ran, their young but rapidly maturing bodies and legs strained against their few remaining limitations. It was as if they understood their playfulness would last only until they reached maturity and were consigned to whatever labor awaited them.

But for that moment, they were free. Perspiration glistened off their lean and muscular bodies as they shoved against each other—competitive, yet companions of heart and spirit.

That vision came rushing at me as I looked out at my friends. It was a thrilling revelation, and as I scooted through the gate and ran toward the group, I had an extra surge in my stride.

The players were caught up in their competition. I had to stand aside until someone scored or the ball changed hands via a turnover. Larry, Pete, Allan, Mike, and Marv were there, along with several others from the varsity and JV teams. Larry's neighbors and friends, Skip Carstensen from St. Patrick's, the Catholic high school in town, and Tom Wisdom, a year older, were there as well.

Watching the contest, my attention was naturally drawn to my classmates. Larry was one of the smaller players, but he stood out from the others as if a spotlight was on him. Only 5' 8", he was solidly built and moved like a deer. No one out there could touch him. He was capable and confident. As a junior, he would go into next football season as the team's headliner at offensive and defensive halfback.

Even though I fully appreciated his abilities, I couldn't quite put a finger on what it was he had athletically that separated him so definitively from the rest of us.

And I couldn't think about Larry without also thinking of his family, especially his parents, Ed and Bernadine. Their nurturing had helped me understand what it meant to be part of the school and sports scene in North Platte.

The chaotic Wachholtz home was like a small municipality. Groups of kids were always coming and going. Staying overnight with Larry in that environment was like visiting a candy factory.

The household was constantly awash in sports. His older sister was a varsity cheerleader, and his younger sister was a member of the Pep Club. His two older brothers, Butch and Kenny—both graduated—had been star athletes in their own right for North Platte varsity teams.

Larry carried a heavy mantle of expectations with grace and without any sign of pressure. Someone else in his situation could have

Left: Larry Wachholtz; *Right:* Pete Tatman

been prideful and condescending. I liked him all the more because he was humble and welcoming, while at the same time a rough-and-tumble character full of fun.

As I shifted my attention from Larry to Pete, I felt I was seeing him for the first time. Pete, nearly six feet tall, was built differently from most of us whose legs were stronger than our upper bodies. His torso was broad and muscular.

Pete had always been an enigma to me. I thought he hung with the wrong crowd and was lackadaisical when it came to sports. Even though I hardly knew him, I had decided I didn't like him. But apparently I was alone with that opinion. He was very popular in school and one of the few of us comfortable around girls.

And he was anything but lazy as I watched him. He was fast, powerful, and graceful at the same time. I was shocked. And I wasn't the only person who was impressed. The other players were showing a lot of respect to him. Even the upperclassmen treated him with unusual deference.

Allan Whitesel

I wasn't sure what to make of my new observation.

It would have been hard to take my eyes off Pete, but all of a sudden Allan made a nice catch right in front of me. Leave it to Whitesel to make his presence known.

As unfamiliar as I was with Pete, I was that well acquainted with Allan. In sports, probably the two positions leading to the closest personal relationship are pitcher and catcher. They see each other at their best and worst, and there is no room for pretension. In our baseball seasons together, I had been one of the team's pitchers and Allan was the catcher. He always said he had to play the catcher position because one leg was shorter than the other, which would have caused him to bounce too much if chasing a grounder or fly ball.

We knew each other inside and out. Allan wore his emotions on his face, as it would turn beet red at the slightest provocation. I could tell by the way he fidgeted behind the plate with fistfuls of dirt what he was thinking. I knew by what he yelled at me between pitches whether he thought I was slacking off or needed encouragement because my best stuff wasn't working.

Mike Kirkman

Through it all, Allan and I became close. He accepted my teasing, and I grew comfortable with his feisty intensity.

Allan wasn't an athlete of Larry's caliber, but no one ever got his number, either. He got as much out of his potential as anyone could. He just kept coming at you with whatever he had left to give. If I had been required to pick any word to describe Allan in an athletic sense, it would have been *relentless*.

I transferred my attention to Mike Kirkman. I couldn't remember ever being at a neighborhood group game when Mike wasn't a part of it. With his easily identifiable widow's peak, he was the epitome of being a Bulldog in the true sense of our school's mascot. If he grabbed onto something, he never gave it up.

He was one who seemed all I was not. While I was reserved, Mike was always in the thick of our school's social activities. He was outgoing and admired by all of the students—just what you would expect from our class president.

His father was the advertising manager for the local paper, the *Telegraph-Bulletin*. Perhaps because of that connection, Mike seemed to

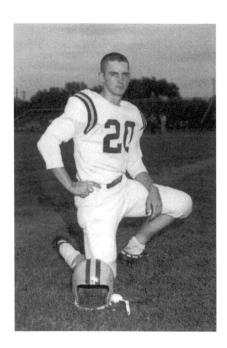

Marv Binegar

know everyone and everything. As someone who knew few adults in town and little of the goings-on, I was impressed by that one characteristic about him alone.

As I in turn observed Marv, I smiled. I had not expected to see him because he lived a few miles away and did not have a car. I was glad he came, though. We had become friends as a result of being on the track team together, and I had developed a lot of respect for him the way he ran the middle distances. Slightly built, he was in every way a real gut-check guy.

Interrupting my daydreaming, someone yelled, "Thomas, we scored, so get in here. You're with the shirts." That put me on same team as Tatman and Kirkman.

As we started playing, I was surprised at how disruptive it was to the ebb and flow of the competition to get me incorporated into the mix. Several plays went by before we all seemed to lose ourselves in the game.

Just when everyone had settled back into the contest, I heard, "Uh-oh."

Raising my eyes toward the voice, I saw a couple of players' fingers point to the gateway where I had come in. A man was entering. I had never seen him before. Trying to seem nonchalant as we continued our match, I warily watched him.

He walked across the north end zone, stopped, patted the white, cast-iron goalpost almost affectionately, then continued to the west side of the cinder track. He purposefully made his way toward the stadium seats. He had a massive black patch slung over his right eye. Who was this guy? Who did he think he was—a pirate or something?

The stranger stopped and leaned back against the chain-link fence between the bleachers and the track, never taking his eyes off us. Although he was studying us, he exhibited no signs of concern about our being on the field. Gradually I took my attention off him and fully reentered our competition.

Then, sensing something, I looked up. There he was, standing next to me on my left. Everyone had stopped playing and was looking intently at him. Trying hard to tear my eyes from staring at the cloth covering his eye socket nearest me, I wondered if that eye was missing or just injured.

I quickly scoped him out. He wasn't as old as my parents. He had a modified crewcut. He was almost my height but built more like Pete, with a muscular body barely contained by his shirt and tie under a sport coat. He had a stern demeanor.

Turning my head to look around at the others, I could see his imposing stature had thrown them off their usual youthful bravado. Were we about to get kicked off the field? Punished?

A deep, powerful voice erupted out of the rugged face atop a ramrod-straight column of a body. "Hello, boys, I'm Crump Redding, your new head football coach. Gather in here."

In the first surprised seconds after he introduced himself, no one spoke as they moved in. I saw a few nods of acknowledgment, but that was it.

The new coach took up the slack. "I'm looking forward to coaching you boys next fall. I know you've had some tough seasons here in recent years, but I can guarantee we'll win more next year than we lose. Tell me your names and what positions you played last year."

He looked to his left, whereupon one by one in a clockwise direction, each player introduced himself. When Larry spoke, Mr. Redding's eyebrows raised and a tight smile appeared on his face. He obviously had heard of Larry.

Coach George "Crump" Redding

Thanks to the introductions, I learned the identity of the one player I hadn't known. I had assumed he was someone's friend, visiting from out of town. He announced himself as Gary Scheet and told Mr. Redding he was going to be a senior. Gary also told his new coach he played tackle, which made sense to me. He was muscular, good sized, and had that tough intensity of a lineman.

The other responses and interchanges went smoothly until it came to me.

With my height of 6' 3" and weight of 180 pounds, I must have appeared to him to be a football player. But when I told him I was not, he growled, "Now you are!"

I thought, Yeah, sure. I don't think so.

With the introductions completed, the new coach started to leave and then turned back.

"I want to add one more thing. You boys had better get in shape over the summer and stay that way, or else my two-a-days in August will kill you!"

We watched him stride away and out the gate. When we were certain he could no longer hear us, everyone started chattering.

"That guy is our new coach? He looks pretty tough."

"He looks like he could take us all at one time!"

"I don't think football is going to be much fun next fall."

"Can you believe his eye patch? I wonder if it's for real or just show."

"Hey, Thomas, great to hear you're going out for football again!"

"Yeah, Bob, aren't you glad you showed up today?"

I didn't find their teasing humorous. Nothing had happened to change my mind about football.

I was glad he was their problem and not mine. I figured I could sleep deep and easy that night, free of any football-related concerns.

4

Seed

Normally a good sleeper, I was surprised I didn't rest well the night of meeting the school's new football coach.

I didn't want to attribute my tossing and turning to him, as he meant nothing to me. At the same time, I felt he posed some sort of threat, even though I couldn't articulate my sense of foreboding. I just knew I was glad I was getting out of town for the summer, far from this undefined peril.

After I downed some cereal and began to clean my dishes, I heard a heavy knock-knock. Looking out, I saw an old, light-green Chevy in the driveway. I did not recognize the car.

I opened the door and was stunned to see Mr. Redding standing on our doorstep.

What was he doing there? No coach or teacher had ever been to my home. It was as foreign to me as if the governor had stopped by to say hello.

I pushed open the screen door.

He dodged the opening door but didn't enter.

"Hello, Bob. I met you yesterday. I'm Crump Redding, North Platte's new football coach." I thought his introduction ironic, as though I could have forgotten him.

"Come on. Take a walk with me so we can talk."

I wanted to close the door and forget he had come. Instead, I

25

followed him. We got as far as the driveway, when he stopped and leaned back against his car.

My senses were on full alert.

"Tell me about North Platte. Does the town support its public high school's athletics?"

I wondered what was behind his small talk, but I followed his lead. "Mr. Redding, I have not lived in North Platte for long. I only moved here at the beginning of seventh grade.

"But as far I know, the whole town is very supportive of our varsity athletic programs, even in football where we have had little success over the years. The stands are always filled, and there is plenty of talk about the games, both before and after."

"What about the business community here?"

"The stores downtown are great, but I don't know many businessmen. A lot of my friends have fathers who are railroaders. The Union Pacific Railroad has a huge operation here."

As I visualized the expansive railroad network, I thought there was a lot more I could tell him. Nestled into the crux of the joining of the east-flowing North and South Platte Rivers, our town of 20,000 was split by the two adjacent east-west arteries of the railroad and Highway 30.

The downtown and the majority of the town's population were located on the south side of the divide. The north side of the railroad was intentionally referred to as *the other side of the tracks*. But I knew he would soon learn all that.

As if he had read my mind, he asked, "How active is your downtown area?"

"Thursday nights and the weekends are the busiest. On Thursday nights, I think everyone in town, young and old alike, and most of the farmers and ranchers and their families from miles around must go downtown. You'll see everyone you know there."

He hadn't asked, but I could have also told him I was finally starting to feel at home in North Platte. For most of us kids, it was a wonderful time and place to be young, growing up safe and sound in essentially one large neighborhood.

Billowing snow blizzards in winter and sweltering heat waves in late summer increased the enjoyment of the fragrant and visually stimulating seasons of spring and fall. Street-covering canopies of giant maples, oaks, and sycamores throughout town not only signaled each seasonal change with their colors and discharge of either new seedlings or dying leaves, but you could also smell the transitions.

No matter. He had already changed the subject.

"What do your parents do?"

"My stepfather is a traveling salesman for the Bowman Biscuit Company, and my mother is a bookkeeper for Hoover Jewelry."

"How about you?" Mr. Redding continued. "What do you do during the summer? Work? Play ball?"

"When I first moved here, I played baseball all summer. I loved it. But two years ago, I started working at a big cattle ranch up north in the Sandhills. For part of the summer I do general ranch work, but most of the time I'm involved in the haying season. In fact, I leave for the ranch tomorrow."

While I was listening and talking, my mind was in high gear fretting over why he had come. I knew he was not in our driveway to talk about North Platte. I kept hoping Mom would come out of the house to send me on some errand, rescuing me from this man.

He got to the point. "Why on earth aren't you playing football? I've got to return home today to get my family ready for our move, so I want to settle this matter here and now."

It was not going to be easy telling this powerful man something he wouldn't want to hear.

"Uh, like I said, football has been a nothing sport in North Platte. The varsity hasn't had a good team in ages."

He lowered his head.

I pushed on, "Plus, I'm not very good. I started at end on the freshman team, but I don't think I played very well."

He lifted his head and gazed down the street over my left shoulder. It didn't seem like he was listening.

I knew I needed another reason for him. I had one, but hadn't wanted to say it.

"On top of that, I didn't like football at all when I played."

He looked at his hands and rubbed them together. I was certain he was not paying any attention to me.

"Do you like sports?"

"Absolutely!"

"Then there has to be some reason other than what you've told me as to why you're not playing."

So he *had* been listening. I hadn't known how to explain my overriding commitment to basketball, but I had to give it a try.

"Over a year ago our freshman basketball team signed a pledge to Coach Smith we would win a state basketball championship by the time we graduate. We call the pledge 'State by '63!' and I feel a huge personal commitment to it. I plan to use the fall off-season again to get better prepared for basketball. And I wouldn't want to risk a football injury that would prevent me from playing basketball."

"Hmmm," he murmured, looking down again.

I was half surprised he didn't rip out my tongue for my blasphemous preference for basketball.

His eyebrows squeezed together inquisitively in a frown, and he looked back at me.

"Smith? He left, didn't he?"

He then straightened up, and I stepped back reactively.

"Yes, but I still feel that obligation."

Before my eyes, he transformed from a friendly conversationalist to an intense advocate in full-on "coach mode." I had seen other coaches attempt to enter that role with their body language, but this man was the first one I had ever seen pull it off. His facial features and entire being changed into a sculpted boulder. He was rock hard. After a short silence, he rumbled, "Do you know anyone who has won a state championship?"

I shook my head.

"I've won one. And I did it in an out-state town in Kansas just like you have here. We took on and beat all those big-city schools in the eastern part of the state.

"Winning a state championship is not easy, and it takes a lot more than wanting it or promising it in some letter. I'll show you how it's done and teach you some of the basics that hold true for success in any sport. I promise going out for football will help you achieve your goal rather than interfere with it."

Out of a combination of pride, rebelliousness, and not having any more arguments, I stood my ground.

"Thanks, Mr. Redding, but—"

"Bullshit. You owe it to yourself to go out next fall. I have to leave now, but I'll see you out there in pads when practice starts. You'll be playing end both ways, so you'd better get yourself in shape. Run a bunch of wind sprints and do some calisthenics up there on the ranch, or the two-a-days will kill you."

I had heard that warning before.

He reached out and shook my right hand, squeezing it so hard my knuckles stung. As I flexed my fingers in pain, Mr. Redding was already getting into his car. Without any eye contact, he backed out of our driveway, turned east toward town, and was on his way.

I stood there, trying to look like a grown-up who had stood up to Mr. Redding, rather than some boy who got overpowered. I was upset with myself for not resolving this matter in my favor. But I still held the cards. I was not going to play football next year or any year, for that man or any other. I was angry with Mr. Redding for assuming I would.

I had no intention of taking running shoes to the ranch to keep in shape. I'd show him. And I definitely had no intention of fulfilling his foolhardy assumption of my participation on his team. Instead I'd have all fall during his precious football season to get in shape for basketball.

● ● ●

A few weeks later, in the gathering dusk unique to sunsets in the Nebraska Sandhills, I asked myself, Am I nuts, or what?

Against all my certainties I would never again play football, I had started running nightly sets of wind sprints after milking the cows.

The first two nights of running, I pretended I was not making any new commitment. I knew I did not like football. That much was definite. I also knew I did not like being told to do something I had drawn a line in the sand against doing. That was clear to me.

Yet there was something enticing about being wanted. And Mr. Redding was right—I liked sports in general. Further, I missed the thrill of playing in official games in front of a crowd.

So by the third night, I had to admit with much self-consciousness that the seed Mr. Redding planted had started to germinate. And by the end of my first week of exercising in the cool of the early evenings, I was mentally a full-fledged football player again.

As I ran the wind sprints, I must have made quite a sight for the other ranch hands as they walked to the main house for dinner, given all of the good-natured insults and jibes they tossed at me. In any event, they were happy to have a head start on the family-style servings before I attacked the remaining food on the table with my ravenous appetite.

No one could have thought I looked more ridiculous than I felt. I tried to run back and forth between the bunkhouse and the barn fast enough so the resulting breeze would blow my straw cowboy hat off my head, but my high-heeled, stiff leather-soled cowboy boots caused me to slip with every stride.

In the diminishing twilight, the barnyard animals were the only ones who heard my frequent curses directed at Mr. Redding.

5

Two-A-Days

Early Fall, 1961

Even though I had arrived back home from the ranch only the night before, it was easy to get up in time for the first morning of two-a-days. When my alarm clock rang at six o'clock, I was already awake.

I was worried over my level of conditioning. I knew I had not prepared myself sufficiently. I feared I was in for a physical nightmare. My stomach felt like it was in my throat.

Knowing we were supposed to be on the practice field by seven o'clock, I got to the school before six-thirty. I had no idea what to expect. Even guys like Larry who had played the previous year didn't feel knowledgeable when I had called them for insight and advice.

The early morning darkness added to my sense of foreboding. As aspiring football players ahead of me entered the back locker-room door, the burst of light from the open door lit the surrounding area for a moment, then all turned black again.

I bumped shoulders quietly with a couple of guys to say hello and then entered the building to begin a new relationship with my old nemesis—football.

"Thomas, what are you doing here? I thought you weren't going out for football anymore." Allan confronted me loud enough for everyone to hear, so I knew he was pulling my chain. I gave him a dirty look.

"Bob, over here. Here's an empty locker, next to mine," Marv yelled at me.

I laid claim to it, noticing names handwritten on adhesive tape indicated Jerry James's locker was on the other side of me, and Mike Kirkman's was across from me. They had not arrived yet, and I hadn't seen Larry, either.

Marv told me to go to the equipment room to pick up my practice gear. Along the way, I looked for other familiar faces. I saw the new guy in town, Gary Scheet, and waved hello.

I knew Jim States would not be here. He still had not received the doctor's approval to play football because of breaking his wrist two years before, so he and Darrel both were skipping football again to practice basketball. But apparently Jim Huffman had decided to go out for football after sitting out one season, like I had. I had seen him at the far end of my aisle when I first came in.

Passing the coaches' office, I observed it was empty. Where was Mr. Redding?

After being given an armload of equipment by the student managers, I went back to my locker. Dumping it all inside, I noticed a sheet of paper stuck in the door. I grabbed it and saw it was titled *Practice Schedule*.

10 minutes:	calisthenics
5 minutes:	wind sprints
5 minutes:	downfield blocking (using wide boards)
8 minutes:	half-speed tackling for technique
5 minutes:	full-speed tackling for contact
7 minutes:	one-on-one blocking
5 minutes:	two-on-one blocking
20 minutes:	install/practice offensive or defensive plays
10 minutes:	dummy scrimmage
10 minutes:	full scrimmage
5 minutes:	wind sprints

Doing a quick addition, I was pleasantly surprised it totaled only ninety minutes. I was also comforted to discover the drills were in small chunks of time. All in all, it didn't appear to be difficult. My stomach inched its way back down to its normal position.

It felt good to be in a locker room again, though there was lots of nervous laughter and teasing going on—about my coming out for the team, about the new coach, about what was going to happen to us. I could tell I wasn't the only one who was apprehensive.

Marv hit me on my butt and told me to get my ass in gear. As I sorted through the equipment I had been given, my most immediate problem was I couldn't get suited up on my own. Everything was different from the stuff we had worn in junior high.

Out of the corners of my eyes, I watched those who played before and tried to emulate them as they assembled loose pads into their pants to protect their thighs and knees and inserted loose pads into a girdle to wear under the pants to protect their hips. Finally, I got the hang of it.

I then assumed I knew how to put on my shoulder pads, but I was wrong. At first, I couldn't distinguish the front from the back.

At least I knew how to put on my jersey and my helmet. But I was shocked at how heavy the helmet was. How would I wear that headpiece for long periods of time?

As I scanned the others after they donned their uniforms, I smiled to myself at how cartoonish they all looked. Did I look that funny?

As it neared seven o'clock, I joined up with Marv, Jerry, and Mike as everyone started to wander out of the locker room. Larry stepped through the door just ahead of me, so I pushed him.

He feigned a big stumble, turned, and welcomed me. "Hey, it's good to see you. You look fit now from your summer's work, but I want to see you in a couple of hours."

Along with Larry, I quietly joined the slow-moving flow as we sauntered over to the practice fields behind the junior-high building.

Ahead in the distance, beneath the backside of the stadium, I saw Mr. Redding. He had a baseball hat on and was wearing a sweatshirt. There were a couple of men with him I didn't recognize. Our gaggle turned toward where they were standing.

Blowing his whistle forcefully several times, the new coach

North Platte's Public Junior (*right front*) and Senior (*left front*) High School buildings and athletic fields

motioned for us to hustle up and gather around him. I saw he wasn't wearing an eye patch. Studying his face in the dim light, I could not determine if he had a glass eye under his glasses.

When we were assembled to his satisfaction, he addressed us in that deep, raspy voice I remembered so vividly.

"Boys, my name is Crump Redding. *Coach* Redding to you. My assistant coaches here are Joe Folsom and Ray Best, along with JV coaches Larry Roth, Dick Johnson, and Floyd Coleman."

Joe Folsom. So this was our new basketball coach. I would not have recognized him from the times we played Ogallala. He was shorter than Coach Smith and didn't look like a basketball player. I wondered what he would be like as an assistant football coach and if I would like him.

Coach Redding's voice powered through my distraction. "My assistants will help me teach you some football and make certain you give me one hundred percent.

"Welcome to the start of our two-a-days. We have to get ready for our first game with Sidney in just a few weeks. Right now, you are only

Coach George
"Crump" Redding

boys. But if you are still wearing those costumes at the end of the season for me, you will be well on your way to becoming men.

"What you've done or not done in the past for the North Platte Bulldogs means nothing right now. Every starting position is wide open, and those who want that honor will have to work hard for it and prove it to me on each and every play."

Since I hadn't played the year before, his challenge to the team didn't bother me, but I wondered how all the guys who did play last year felt. In basketball I certainly felt entitlement as a returning player.

As he removed his sweatshirt, I studied our new coach. His T-shirt was tight on his chiseled upper body. His hands looked like baseball mitts. He kept digging his football cleats at the sparse turf as he talked. He looked just as fearsome as how I remembered him in my driveway—like he could tear out my heart either by reaching down my throat or up my ass.

Why the hell did I let him intimidate me or motivate me or whatever into playing football again? I couldn't believe I was actually standing there.

I snapped back to the present as Coach Redding cut through the fog in my head. "One thing I believe with all my heart is each of you is critical to the success of the team. The reason is simple. If you are the lowest ranked member of the team and you improve, you force everyone above you to make even more progress. I only want players on my squad who recognize and accept that responsibility. Each of you will equally bear the burden of how successful this team can become.

"You were given a description of how every practice session will be run. Ninety minutes—no more, no less—so I expect you to give me everything you've got. I will not tolerate loafing from anyone at any time.

"At this moment, I'm sure you're just like every team I've met for the first time. You think ninety minutes doesn't seem so long. But you've never spent an hour and a half with me. I developed these abbreviated sessions because on my first coaching job in Grenola, Kansas, I had several players who had to take the early after-school bus so they could get back to their families' farms in time for chores before darkness. I've kept using them because I found them to be perfect for maintaining effort and focus.

"Every exercise is designed to replicate game situations, so you'll come to discover you have a leg up on our competition. After going through my practices, you'll find the actual games are easy. That is, if you survive the practices!"

I was thinking, Who is he kidding? Survive ninety minutes of piecemeal exercises? This'll be a piece of cake.

As I made eye contact with Larry, he nodded confidently as if he had read my mind.

Blowing his whistle, Coach Redding started indoctrinating us into his disciplined routine. We found ourselves launched into his football universe.

"Line up in rows ten-players-wide facing me. Give yourself plenty of room between one another and between your rows because you'll be spending a lot of time on the ground.

"Co-captains, you were voted in last year to lead your teammates, so get up front and face them. Listen closely, because you'll be expected to run calisthenics each practice for the rest of the season."

Coach Redding waited for them to get situated, then started again. "First, jumping jacks. You should know how to do them, so get going." His whistle blew for us to begin.

"Faster, faster! Keep it up! Keep in rhythm with the person in front of you. You guys look like you've never done anything together as a team before."

My shoulders felt like they were going to explode as my arms fought my shoulder pads every time I clapped my hands overhead. When was this going to stop? After what seemed like a long time, I didn't think I could jump and spread my legs one more time.

"Is this too hard for you weaklings? Kick those legs out! If you need me to help you get them spread out just let me know, and I'll step in right behind you and kick them out for you."

A whistle blew for us to stop. I thought the entirety of calisthenics was only supposed to be ten minutes long. That one exercise seemed like ten minutes by itself.

Oh, God, another whistle.

"Listen up! Next up is running in place, but every time I blow my whistle, I want you to fall to the ground on your stomach and bounce right back up and keep running.

"Watch me. I'll show you how it's done. Coach Best, blow your whistle when you want me to fall to the ground."

Coach Redding started madly running in place with his arms in a cocked position. His eyes were glazed with intense focus, and dust flew up from his stomping cleats. Coach Best blew his whistle, and Coach Redding dove for the ground on his stomach and in one motion was back up on his feet again, running in place. How did he do that?

Coach Best blew his whistle again, and Coach Redding fell into his dust cloud once more and exploded back up, running hard. He stopped, breathing normally. As my stomach started lurching its way upward again, I knew this was not going to be any fun at all.

"Start on my whistle." It shrilled, and we began running in place. "Faster, faster! Let's go! Look up! What are you looking at the ground for?"

A blast from his whistle, and we unevenly fell to the ground and more unevenly struggled to our feet.

"What was that? You guys aren't football players! Try it again." One whistle after another sounded.

"Together! Dive for the ground and bounce back up together! You're supposed to be a team."

The gawdammed whistle again. And again. And again.

Mud formed inside my helmet as the dust liquefied from my sweat. It oozed down my entire head and neck. The inside of my head felt like mud, too. I didn't think I could do another one of those "ups and downs."

I snuck a peek at Larry to see how he was doing and was gratified to see him bent over trying to catch his breath.

"Let's keep going! Harder, harder! Together! Run in synch with each other. At least try to look like a team."

Finally he called for us to stop. The co-captains looked like they were about to die. How long had we been doing this? Was it time to quit practice yet?

"Push-ups! Get down and give me twenty quick push-ups!" His whistle . . .

"Oh, my God! What are you goofballs doing?" His whistle again. "Stop! Get up and watch me do a proper push-up."

He dropped to the ground. With a straight and rigid body he fired off ten quick and powerful push-ups. He was a physical freak.

He blew his whistle for us to try again. And again. He made us do three sets of twenty. Was he crazy? Most of us couldn't get our body off the ground during the last couple of sets, but he kept on yelling at us. Unbelievable.

"OK, get up. In a week or so you'll be doing one hundred push-ups easily. You now get a little break with some leg lifts. You will lie on your back with your hands under your butt and then raise your feet and legs.

"On my whistle you'll spread your legs wide and hold them there. On my next whistle bring them together again and hold them. You'll repeat that until my double whistle, when you can drop your legs until the next set.

"Three sets. Ready? On the ground, now, feet forward."

His whistle blew and immediately blew again. "You idiots! I said on your backs!"

By the third set, my legs were burning and shaking. I thought maybe he wouldn't notice if I rested one leg at a time on the ground.

"You there. Thomas, is it? Stop loafing! Raise both legs!"

"OK, ladies, on your feet! Let's finish off with a nice long set of running in place again. I know how much you enjoyed that earlier."

After what seemed like an eternity and an infinite number of whistles, Coach Redding stopped us. "OK. That was your warm-up. Let's get started on practice and learn some football."

The rest of the ninety minutes dissolved into a pain- and fatigue-induced haze. I'd never been that sore and tired. Finally he blew his whistle for the millionth time and called us together around him.

"Be back here at this spot at five o'clock, ready to go. I never want to see you walking to and from practice again. You dragged yourselves out here this morning like you were mourners at a funeral. I'll never witness a sorry sight like that again, or you'll be the ones who are dead. Hustle out here like you have something you love to do.

"Right now, race each other back to the showers and wash off that good, healthy Nebraska dirt. Clean out the inside of your helmet and shake off your equipment. Take good care of everything. You'll be living in those clothes for a while."

One last whistle of the morning.

"Go!"

I ran as hard as I could, but my legs felt like fence posts. I was sure Coach Redding must be right on my tail, ready to blow his whistle in my ear for loafing again.

We all bunched together as we tried to squeeze through the door at the same time. No one said a word. I plopped on the bench in front of my locker. I thought I might have to shower with my practice gear on. I didn't have the energy to take anything off.

Finally I returned to a minimal form of life. Looking around at the other weary aspirants, I understood why Redding had warned us about his two-a-days. Everybody was dragging, and their elbows, knuckles, and shins looked like mine. It was as if they had been put through a meat grinder.

At least my pads came off easier than they went on. Would my legs get me all the way to the showers?

The pounding shower was heaven. I finally felt like I made it back to the living and could walk home.

"What do you think?" I asked Larry, who, standing next to me, was also recovering under a stream of water.

"It's hard to tell," he responded. "It's always a struggle to get in shape for a new sport. I'm impressed, though, at Coach Redding's physical abilities. He must be forty years old or more. If he can get the team to be as capable as he is, that'll be a good start."

"He's an animal," I answered. Then, changing the subject, "I was surprised to see our new basketball coach out there today."

Larry answered, "I don't think that's unusual. Smith was an assistant last year under Easter. I didn't recognize Folsom, though, and I still can't believe Smith is gone."

I agreed. "What a bunch of crap that was."

We left it at that and went back to our lockers to dry off and get dressed.

Coach Folsom was the least of my problems. I had to be back by five o'clock, ready to go, for the second session with Coach Redding.

Heaven help me.

6

Morons

Many blossoming bruises, festering blisters, and oozing sores later, we completed the two-a-days.

I had survived. My puny wind sprints on the ranch over the summer had hardly prepared me for the two-a-days, but the dual workouts had forced me into the best physical condition I had ever been in.

To my surprise, we were executing our calisthenics in a crisp and synchronous manner. An even greater shock was the satisfaction I felt. I would never have guessed a well-harmonized physical exercise could provide almost as much satisfaction as a well-executed series of plays in a real game.

None of us had ever seen or experienced anything like Coach Redding. What a fanatic. I had learned he did wear a glass eye, but even though he had only one good eye, he made up for that by apparently possessing optical receptors all over his body. He could see someone trying to sneak a breather even when his back was turned.

As school began, we segued into one practice a day, but Coach Redding's whistle was still a factor. It constantly interrupted the proceedings and was always followed by some high-volume criticism from him.

Without fail, any time one of us missed a block or tackle in one of his drills, Coach Redding tossed the other player aside and jumped in without pads opposite the offending player to show him how to make the play. It usually resulted in a quick trip to the dirt and a new lesson implanted deep in a new bruise, even if only to the ego.

Coach's obscenity-laced talk and physical interaction didn't sit comfortably with everyone, especially some of the seniors who had been fond of Coach Easter. Most of us, however, were too tired and intimidated to worry about it.

We couldn't even gang up on him. In one early scrimmage, Coach had the quarterback step aside so he could show him how he wanted him to execute a pass play.

Byron Boslau, a senior offensive guard, saw his opportunity to get back at the coach for those "lessons." Byron let a defensive player slip by him who then, as planned, "accidentally" ran into Coach Redding for a bit of payback, knocking him solidly to the ground.

Coach Redding picked himself up, not saying a word or acknowledging being hit. He went back a few yards and bent over, waiting for the offensive huddle to form around him. As it did, he reached over and popped Boslau so hard on his shoulder pads he fell into a backwards somersault. As Byron rolled over and returned sheepishly to the huddle, Coach Redding harshly admonished him, "Don't *ever* let anyone through that line when I'm playing quarterback!"

Looking around the huddle at everyone's astonished faces, I was convinced Coach would forever be safe.

For me, even though it was the first activity after calisthenics, the pivotal point of each session was the downfield-blocking drill. It was a monster, and Coach Redding monitored every move we made. Every practice component afterwards seemed easy by comparison.

For that drill, we collected into five single-file lines. The first person in each line ran forward down the varying lengths of foot-wide boards. The flat plank forced us to run with our feet spread wide, promoting balance and the ability to turn easily in either direction. At the end of each board, the player pivoted at a right angle in a pre-assigned direction and then ran straight ahead again to throw a cross-body block on his respective lane's blocking dummy held by one of the coaches or a manager.

The inside lane had the shortest board and the shortest overall distance to its blocking dummy. The total distance to be run increased with each lane to the outside.

The natural inclination after performing the drill a couple of times was to crowd into the one or two inside lanes with the shortest lengths. Because of that, if you went into one of the outside lanes, so few players were there you barely got back to the line before it was your turn to go again. But I found it was worth going through extra physical punishment rather than taking all the crap Coach Redding gave me when I wimped out and took the inside lanes.

One player who always took the far outside lane was Pete.

I was getting to know him better, which was all it took to think more highly of him. He was a good guy, clearly in love again with football. He remarked several times how for the first time in a long time, football was uncomplicated and fun again. I think Pete had needed Coach Redding's discipline and relished his constant measuring of each of us against tough standards and against each other.

Pete weighed somewhere in the neighborhood of 165–170 pounds, but hitting him was like smashing into a cement wall. In full-speed tackling drills, we all hated to tackle or be tackled by Pete, as the contact usually guaranteed our seeing stars for several minutes. It was easy to understand why the upperclassmen had been so respectful toward him that day playing touch football on the varsity field when we first met Coach Redding.

Talking to Larry after practice one day, we had a good laugh about one incident involving Pete. Alan Kehr, a small-framed but brave defender, had done what the coaches yelled at him to do on a kick-coverage drill. He attempted to force Pete to run to the inside where more tackling help was available.

But Pete decided he wanted to go to the outside and probably didn't know he ran over Alan when he changed course. We thought Pete had killed him. Alan slowly picked himself off the ground and wobbled to the sidelines. The next day, Alan was happily engaged as one of the team's student managers.

Many of us subsequently had similar collisions with Pete, but only one opening had been available for student manager, and Alan got there first.

Larry offered up, "There will be a lot of players we go against this year who will want to switch over to student manager when Pete runs over them." I nodded heartily in agreement.

Then Larry shifted the subject. "You know, I really like Coach Redding."

I was surprised because Coach displayed no extra respect or consideration to Larry.

"He knows what he's talking about, and I appreciate how all of his drills replicate game situations. I love the competition he creates among us, and I particularly like his ability to distinguish and take action against any slackers. We needed that in the past."

Listening to Larry helped me put the new coach in perspective, as I had no other reference point.

"I do worry about Coach Redding's total emphasis on defense, though," Larry continued. "He's so consumed with our defense, I'm concerned there won't be enough time to learn whatever offense he will want us to use. We have less than two weeks to go before our first game."

My head had been spinning so fast, I hadn't noticed the omission. When I thought about it, though, the only discussion I could remember Coach Redding having with us related to our offense was regarding point-after-touchdown attempts, or PATs as he called them. He had told us that his teams had never kicked their PATs, and neither would we. He said he felt much more confident running the ball—he believed the percentages favored the run over the kick.

As the days kept passing, I observed more and more townspeople showing up for our practices. Mike's father—Jim Kirkman—was a manager at the local newspaper, and also wrote a weekly column. Mike Smith was the sports editor, and together they had been penning optimistic assessments of the new coach in town and of our team.

The same occurred with Joe di Natalie, who handled sports for the town's radio station. The three of them had done a good job with their audiences, building interest and curiosity about our team.

Through one of Kirkman's articles, I learned the reasons Coach Redding was taking so long to install the offense that Larry was impatient to learn. Coach Redding told Mr. Kirkman he was concerned about our lack of football knowledge and conditioning, consistently poor execution of fundamentals, and small overall team size and insufficient strength.

My only thought was, Is that all? I was prepared to be indignant about his caustic assessment until both Larry and Pete told me they agreed with him.

The same article also described how Coach Redding always had a weight-training program for his previous teams, as he believed even a small player who could lift his own weight could play effectively against players who significantly outweighed him.

That explained why Line Coach Ray Best brought in his personal set of weights and configured part of our locker room into a weight room. While we only spent ninety minutes on the practice field, Coach Redding regularly had us lifting weights before hitting the showers.

The calendar kept advancing, and finally Coach Redding ran out of time. He had no choice but to give us our offensive plays.

Before practice on the Monday before our first game, Coach Redding stepped to the locker room blackboard. All of our previous coaches had used X's and O's to depict defensive and offensive players, respectively. Coach Redding instead used V's and O's because, "With the sharp point of a 'V,' I can pinpoint precisely where I want each defensive player to line up. For example, I can assign a defensive tackle to line up in a slot between two offensive linemen, or on one of their inside or outside shoulders, or directly opposite one of their heads."

To this point, the O's he had used represented only a generic opponent's offensive alignment. On this day, however, as he prepared to lay out the O's in the offensive scheme he had planned for us, he opened with, "Boys, I am going to make this simple. You'd better get this quickly so we can practice these plays over the next few days."

Drawing on the board, he continued, "We're going to run a straight-T offense, with the quarterback over center, and three backs behind him in a tight, straight line parallel to the line of scrimmage. "Each play we call will consist of two numbers. The first number will identify which player will carry the ball." Writing numbers next to the appropriate O's, he continued, "The quarterback will be designated as number 1, the left halfback as 2, the fullback as 3, and the right half as 4.

"The second number will tell where that player will run. On the line, the center location will be the number *0*. We will generally run a balanced line, with two guards on either side of the center, then two tackles, and finally two ends. The spaces between the seven linemen from the quarterback's perspective will be odd numbers to the left of the center—*1, 3,* and *5* from the center out—and even numbers to the right of the center—*2, 4,* and *6,* also from the center out.

"For example, *10* is a quarterback sneak over center." He drew an arrow representing the quarterback running straight ahead.

"A play called as *42* is the right halfback running between the center and the right guard." He drew an appropriate line.

"*33* will be the fullback running between the left guard and tackle," with another line drawn.

"For passes, the left end is considered number *5* and the right end is number *6*. Accordingly, a *15 slant pass* is a toss from the quarterback to the left end, who runs downfield three steps and then cuts inside at a forty-five degree angle. A *46 post pass* will be thrown by the right halfback to the right end, who runs five strides downfield and then turns outside at a forty-five-degree angle." More lines . . .

By the time he finished, there were numbers and lines drawn all over the board, with the lines going in all directions.

"That's as simple as I can make it. If any of you can't count, you can't play. For the rest of you, I'm expecting you to know and understand this system as of right now."

Despite the blackboard's visual overload, I had to admit the concept was straightforward. However, in practice I found it easy to forget my assignments.

We first ran the plays in slow motion and then speeded them up with mixed results. Perhaps not all of us could count, after all.

Over the following days, he tweaked the initial offensive setup he had given us. He moved the backs closer to the line, stating that positioning them in that way would counteract our line's small size by our not having to hold our blocks for a long time.

He and Coach Best also told the interior linemen to widen their spacing gradually throughout a game. The premise was the defensive linemen would follow them outwards, thus creating the beginnings of a hole in the line even before the ball was snapped.

They also introduced us to cross blocking and double-team blocking, with Coach Redding explaining he wanted us to have additional tools to compensate for our physical and skill-related shortcomings. We weren't very good at those techniques, but I could see that once we were, we would have much better success.

• • •

Time passed much too quickly, and before we knew it, it was Thursday night, the night before our first game against the Sidney Maroon. Larry worried aloud, "We need more practice with the offense. We don't have it yet." I had to agree with him. We were not ready. We needed at least another week.

Coach Redding called us together at the end of practice. "Boys, I have someone I want you to meet. The school board just approved a new team-related position. Say hello to Max Byersdorf, your team medical trainer. You'll get to know Max very well. You'll always be acquiring minor injuries of one sort or another, and now we have someone who will help you heal as quickly as possible."

Max was one of those people I instantly liked. He was of average height and build, wore glasses, and had dark, combed hair. He also had a pleasant smile. My intuition was he would be a good friend to us.

Coach Redding then got to the primary subject at hand. "I know you are worried about your first game with those Sidney *Morons*."

Everyone laughed when Coach Redding purposely botched Sidney's real team name, "Maroon." With the laughter, much of our nervousness evaporated.

"Stephenson, you've done a good job in learning your new position at quarterback, and you're ready to lead us into the game.

"The rest of you also know the specific responsibilities of your position. Keep it simple out there. Don't worry about anyone else at this time. Just do your own job and count on your teammates doing theirs.

Coach George "Crump" Redding

"Most of you are playing both ways, which requires a high degree of concentration and commitment. You should be in sufficient physical shape to handle the rigors of both offense and defense, so do not let up mentally at any time.

"For those of you who are playing only on offense or defense or a special team, keep your head in the game at all times and get on the field the instant you are needed. Don't make me have to find you on the sidelines, or I'll spend my energy instead looking for your replacement.

"And no matter what, no one leaves the field at any time without my approval.

"We've just started to get to know each other. You are nowhere near understanding football the way you will by the end of the season. I am, however, generally pleased with the progress you've made and the effort you've put forth so far.

"Even though you've barely scratched the surface of what you can do, go out there tomorrow and start something new for North Platte—the first victory in a winning season!

"Gather together in here. Raise your hands above your team captains. Captains, send them on their way."

We collected around him and yelled "Go!" in unison, and then raced for the showers. We knew the next time we suited up, it would be for real.

7

"Beat Hastings!"

We traveled to Sidney for our first game of the season with high hopes but no way to know how good we were. After the game ended in a 6–6 tie, we still didn't know.

Our starting lineup had consisted of eight seniors and three of us juniors—Larry as a 148-pound halfback, Pete as a 167-pound fullback, and me as a 180-pound end. I finally caught a pass for fourteen yards from Bill Stephenson after earlier catching nothing but a verbal barrage from Coach Redding when I dropped an easy one. Pete was the leading rusher and tackler for the game, making quite a statement for himself.

But the talk in the locker room after the game was all about Larry and his early-game benching by Coach Redding. After only one series of plays, Coach Redding had removed Larry from the game, but most of us didn't know why.

My friend Bruce Kuhlmann had been nearby at the time, so he provided the explanation for all of us eager listeners. "First Coach Redding tells Larry to take off his helmet, that he was through for the game. Larry looked shocked—like he had never been treated like that before." All of us who had been on the field at the time were paying attention to every word.

Bruce went on. "We couldn't believe it, either. We all kept our eyes on Larry as he cooled his heels on the bench. After a while, we noticed

Larry had moved back up on the sideline, trying hard to catch Coach Redding's attention."

Our eyes grew big as the story progressed.

"All of a sudden, Coach motioned for Larry to come over to him. Larry jumped out of his skin, put on his helmet, and buckled his chinstrap. Ready to go back in the game, he ran to Coach Redding to get his instructions."

We nodded knowingly.

"Coach grabbed Larry by the shoulder pads, bent over and looked at him nose to nose, and said, 'Larry, do you know what I've been thinking?'

"Larry answered eagerly, 'No, Coach, what have you been thinking?'

"Coach looked at Larry long and hard." Bruce hesitated for effect. "Then he said, 'Larry, I've been thinking you're a gawdamned chickenshit!'"

We exploded in laughter, coughing and spitting all over ourselves and each other. "What happened then?"

Bruce answered, "You'd better ask Larry."

"Larry, get over here."

Knowing Larry got back in the game, we wondered aloud, "What did you say to Coach after that?"

"Oh, crap, can't we just forget it?" he pleaded.

"No way! What happened next?"

Larry took his time, and then proceeded. "My first thought was, 'Bullshit—*you're* the gawdamned chickenshit!'"

"Oh, my God," someone said as we burst out laughing again. "Is that what you told him?"

Larry smiled for the first time. "No, it wasn't." Continuing, he said, "I stood there a while stewing over what he had said, until I realized he had been right. I had not been playing to my capabilities, and Coach knew it even if I didn't. That guy is some different kind of cat!

"I finally set my pride aside and went back to pitch my case to Coach. I told him I wasn't a 'chickenshit' and asked to be put back in the game to prove it. I guess I convinced him, because he soon let me back in.

"I learned my lesson. This is one coach not to be messed with."

We patted Larry on his back, glad we could learn that lesson through him and not through our own direct encounter.

Given my lackluster performance, though, as that was my first football game in some time, I wondered how the coach missed calling me out as a chickenshit, too.

At least the excitement for football as a team sport showed signs of appearing at long last. Although I didn't feel as if I performed anywhere near my potential, I could for the first time begin to think about what might be possible.

A week later, our second game and our first home game was against Kearney. Both our new offense and steady defense clicked, giving us a 25–0 victory over a relatively inexperienced squad. Pete was again the star both offensively and defensively, with postgame kudos also going to Stephenson and Boslau.

Coach Redding had begun to eliminate ineffective running tendencies he saw in both Pete and Larry. Pete liked to dodge and weave, but Coach Redding always told him, "Pete, just pick out somebody in a different color jersey and run over him! I want dirt flying out of your cleats like a charging bull!"

Larry was just the opposite. Despite a knack for avoiding tacklers, he often chose to bang into someone to mix it up. Coach Redding would then yell, "Dammit, Larry! Don't let those sons-a-bitches touch you!"

Against Kearney, Pete and Larry had finally started to do what he wanted, and it paid off for them and for our team.

We next played a tough Colorado team, Sterling, to another tie, 12–12. Pete was yet again the leading ground gainer, but Larry made the biggest play in the game with a timely thirty-yard interception for a touchdown. He also produced a momentum-shifting punt return at a critical point in the game that led to a score.

Our defense suffered a huge loss, though, when a key defensive halfback, senior Tom Wisdom, broke his collarbone and was told he would be sidelined for the season.

Seeing Tom in the locker room with his shoulder taped up, I teased, "We always figured you would break a leg instead."

Tom smiled wryly. He knew what I meant. Out of the blue during one of the two-a-day practices, Coach Redding had abruptly stopped practice. He grabbed Tom by the pads, yelling, "Wisdom, did you have polio as a child?"

Tom had answered back with a wary and confused look on his face. "No, Coach. Why?"

He had become the perfect straight man for Coach Redding's snarled-out punch line, "Then how come your legs are so skinny?"

With our young season's record at a questionable 1–0–2, we and the whole town were unsure how good or bad a team we were. There was lots of speculation as to whether we were better than our record or just another lousy Bulldog team in a long string of losers.

No one had to wait long to make their decision.

Next up was Hastings, a powerful team populated with several superior athletes. We traveled there expecting a tough battle and were thoroughly rewarded. The halftime score was only 6–0 in their favor, but the second half was a sobering wakeup call for us. The game ended with Hastings having dominated us by the score 32–7.

At that point, with a worsening record of 1–1–2, the honeymoon for the new coach and our team was over. There was no more speculation. The sportswriters and radio announcers were certain we were going to continue the historical pattern of only one to three wins a season. The atmosphere we faced among students, parents, and fans was heavy with resigned despair.

For our first practice after the Hastings game, I was certain Coach Redding would read us the riot act. While getting suited up in our practice gear, the talk in the locker room was reconciled to accepting failure for the season.

Mike told us, "Lots of people stopped by our house over the weekend to tell Dad they have given up on our team. I even got the impression some of them want to go to the school board and complain Coach Redding is not the right man to turn our program around."

I was thinking, This is not what I signed up for. Redding had promised we would be winners, not losers.

Larry confirmed Mike's information. "Coach Redding told my father he had also heard those concerns. But when I asked Dad what he thought, he said Redding was the right man for the job."

When we saw Coach Redding, he was combative. "Forget that shit you're hearing about our football record! Don't listen to anybody but me.

"Take those two ties and put them in the win column and see how you feel about our record.

"Sidney and Sterling are both outstanding teams, and neither one has yet to lose a game. You did well to tie them so early in your getting familiar with what I want from you."

Feeling better about ourselves, we handily won the next two games against Alliance and McCook. With three wins under our belt, we felt like at least a small monkey was off our back, as the negative chatter behind the scenes mostly disappeared.

Then, just as we were on an upward trend, we ran into a buzz saw and got chewed up. Waiting for us on their home turf was Grand Island.

We made a few turnovers to help them, but my overwhelming memory of the game was of Grand Island's offense. They pounded up the middle time and time again with their tough fullback, Stan Farrar. They kept coming at us behind a strong offensive line, anchored by center Dick Luebbe.

Until then, we had been using a defense with four down-linemen with good success. For this game, however, Coach Redding wanted to have more linebacker and secondary flexibility against their reputed strong offense. The week of the game, he instituted a defense with only three down-linemen, centered by a nose guard playing directly opposite the offensive center.

The strategy put the entire weight of our defense on the nose-guard position. With the right athlete and with adequate experience, that position could possibly have created havoc with the execution of their offensive plays. But with only a few days of practice, any player in that role was susceptible to being double-team blocked by the center and either of the guards.

Sure enough, as the game proceeded, our defense crumbled.

From my balcony seat at defensive end, I was entertained throughout the first half by the spectacle of Farrar running off either side of Luebbe through gaping holes up the middle of our line. Grand Island was having a blast without our providing any noticeable resistance.

But the best was yet to come. In the second half, I was moved to a front-row seat. I was one of several people inserted at nose guard in a series of desperate moves to find some personnel combination within our new defense that would work against their double-team blocking.

In my first play at nose guard, I was knocked completely upside-down, only to rise up in time to get a face full of Farrar's knee. I repeated that hapless performance for a few plays, until I was moved aside for some other poor schmuck.

At least when you get your ass whipped and you lose, it hurts less than losing a game you felt you should have won. We players accepted the loss without a lot of judgment.

But the next Monday at practice, unlike after the loss to Hastings, Coach Redding was pissed. I initially figured it might be because he felt at least partially responsible for changing our defense at the last minute.

But he was far removed from taking any responsibility for our destruction. He was determined to teach us "how to play the nose-guard defense correctly."

With the whole team gathered around, our first-string defense repeatedly ran through several plays using that defensive set against our second team's version of the "Grand Island offense." Byron got the honor of being the sacrificial nose-guard stand-in.

After getting himself dusted on his butt over and over, receiving a healthy dose of coaching advice each time, he finally protested in frustration, "It would have been nice to get this much help *before* the game!"

We thought Byron had committed suicide.

After a long, withering look from Coach Redding's one eye, Coach blew his whistle and broke us apart into blocking and tackling drills.

Gary whispered to me, "I don't think we'll ever see that defense again."

Left: Author and Denny Nelson (#41) carry Coach Redding off the field to celebrate our first regular-season winning record in years. *Right:* Other team-mates join in to help carry Coach Redding.

And so it was. With the return of our original four-down-linemen defense and our simple offense, we closed out the regular season with easy victories against Scottsbluff and Gering.

The way we won the last two regular season games provoked a new awareness in me that we were not totally consumed as a team with winning. It was more like we played each game in the same deliberate way we practiced—play by play. When a play worked, that was the way it was supposed to be, and nothing was said. When a play didn't work, Coach Redding yelled at us for all the reasons it didn't, and we moved on. There was no "game" stress. Our pressure was to execute. And execute.

With those two victories, something else occurred. With our questionable season record, achieving any kind of championship was the furthest thing from my mind. Besides, I had never thought much about conference-level championships. In basketball, all I had my eyes on was a state championship.

But with our late-season success, I received a lesson in Nebraska high-school sports. For basketball, conference play had no effect on a state title. Every team in the state, regardless of record, participated in postseason district tournaments to determine the state-tournament playoff teams.

But football had no statewide playoff system. The preeminent sportswriter—Gregg McBride—of the state's top newspaper, the *Omaha World-Herald*, provided the definitive team rankings throughout the year and crowned the state champion at season's end. The Associated Press also named a final champion. The result was that in football, conference play was very influential on a team's ranking.

Our high school was part of the Big Ten conference, consisting of ten Class A non-metro teams to the west of Lincoln and Omaha. Our "out-state" conference had two five-team divisions—East and West. In the next to last weekend of the season, while we were beating Scottsbluff, losses by other teams in our division unexpectedly handed us a West division title.

That wasn't particularly impressive to me, but what did grab my attention was with that honor came a spot in the Big Ten conference championship game. When I realized we had been given that opportunity, I was equal parts shocked and proud. For the first time in many years, most of the state would be interested in a North Platte high-school football game.

Our opponent in the title game would be Hastings, the same powerhouse that manhandled us earlier in the year. But they likewise had backed into their division title. Their dominating East division leader, Grand Island, had inexplicably lost a key game at the end of the season.

We favored playing Hastings instead of Grand Island. Sure, Hastings had soundly beaten us from a scoring standpoint, but Grand Island flat-out thrashed us. By unexpectedly surrendering their conference's title to Hastings, we felt Grand Island had assisted our school for the first time in sports memory.

To capitalize on our team's turnaround, good fortune, and cascading flood of enthusiasm, Joe di Natalie implored his radio audience to answer all personal and business phone calls with the greeting,

"Beat Hastings!"

That was what the townspeople needed—a demonstrable way they could participate. Consequently, all we players heard for days was, "Beat Hastings!" "Beat Hastings!" "Beat Hastings!"

Our fans were crazy with unfamiliar excitement. After years of humiliation, even this year of hope had started out the first few games as if it would contain more disappointment. They were exploding with long-dormant passion.

Sportswriters throughout the state didn't give us much of a chance to win, given our prior substantial loss to Hastings. Plus, our 5–2–2 record was not indicative of a championship-caliber team.

But with a season of Coach Redding's fundamentals and weight-lifting under our belts, we were not the same team Hastings and Grand Island had whipped earlier.

● ● ●

November 10, 1961, provided a crisp, overcast Friday afternoon for the biggest North Platte football game in what seemed forever.

Hastings rolled into North Platte brimming with self-assurance. Our local newspaper reported their coach, Ollie Smith, was warning his players they would be seeing a different team than the one they had crushed 32–7 earlier in the year. But through the Hastings newspaper articles, we could sense their players and fans were supremely confident of the outcome in their favor.

We had classes in the morning, but our teachers were as eager as we were to get the game under way. They let us out early so we could go to the locker room to go through our pregame routine.

We first put on our uniform undergarments, and Max taped our ankles. We then moved to the gymnasium, where in the semi-dark we lay on our backs on gymnastic mats placed on the floor. We quieted our minds. Collected our thoughts. Got balanced. Became focused on the here and now.

After about fifteen minutes, Coach Redding in his usual custom mingled among us softly telling us, "Today is payday. You've worked hard for this. Today you get to collect your check. Today is payday."

Finished wandering through our group laid out like so many bales of hay in a field, he clapped his hands. That signaled us to go back into the locker room to finish suiting up.

We soon were ready. Coach Redding gave his last-minute instructions to the game captains regarding the coin toss and reviewed the first series of offensive plays with us.

It was time to go. As was our custom, we gathered around our coach and began to bounce up and down, chanting, "Go! Go! Go!" We hit our vocal peak and, still loudly chanting, surged out of the locker-room door.

I was amazed by what I saw.

All the cheerleaders were waiting there to lead us to the field through a corridor of Pep Club and Lettermen's Club members stretching from the locker room to the gate. Each one was cheering us on.

Nearing the field, we first heard and then saw the record 4,300 fans on hand to witness the game, including five to six hundred people who had traveled from Hastings to cheer on their team. Both bands were playing as loudly as they could, and everyone was yelling at the top of their lungs. It was easy to recognize how important this game was to both towns and schools.

Our calisthenics were a blur. I was not accustomed to playing in the limelight like this, especially for football. I was barely aware we lost the coin toss and would start the game on defense.

After I kicked off to start the game, Hastings ground out a couple of first downs. We then made them face a fourth and one at their own 48-yard line.

Quarterback Wayne Weber surprised us by gambling with a quarterback sneak. He made the first down to keep their drive alive, solidly establishing their determination and confidence in their first drive of the game.

Hastings proceeded to steadily move the ball down the field until they reached our 12-yard line. Momentum was already on their side.

Our defense stiffened. With key plays by seniors Don Titus and Gary Scheet, we threw them back to the 22-yard line, where we finally took over on downs.

Cheerleaders
escort Bulldogs
to Big Ten
Conference
title game.

Three plays later, we had traveled seventy-eight yards to score, fueled by Larry's two runs of forty-three and thirty-three yards. All of our season-long practice sessions on blocking, especially our five-lane downfield-blocking drills with boards, paid off as we opened huge holes both on the line and downfield for Larry.

Our extra point attempt failed, but we led 6–0. When we left the field for halftime, 6–0 was still the score.

The second half felt like a repeat of the first. Hastings, behind Weber and their fine runner, fullback Jack Giddings, had a few good scoring chances throughout. But whenever Hastings threatened, our defense shut them down.

Near the end of the game, Larry got his second touchdown of the day on a short burst off tackle. That score put the game away for us, but our long scoring drive almost didn't happen.

It was made possible by senior end Denny Nelson, who single-handedly fought for and gathered in our fumble on our 5-yard line at the beginning of our drive. If we had lost that fumble and Hastings had scored, the game could have flipped on us right then and there.

As the game clock ticked down its final seconds, I was far away from the line of scrimmage, having run downfield on a deep pass play. I was in a perfect position to watch all of the cheerleaders, fans, coaches, and players on the sidelines explode out to encircle the rest of my teammates in the middle of the field.

The Hastings players appeared to be in slow motion as they moved off the field toward the visitors' locker room in surprised disappointment. At the same time, our contingent was in high-speed, astonished fulfillment—churning and churning. Everyone was running around with grins and wide-open eyes.

I could finally relax. I'll be damned. We did it! We beat Hastings!

I dropped to my knees, leaned over and kissed the ground in thanks. I had made it through the season without an injury that would have taken me out of basketball.

I jumped back up and raced to the swirling mass of players and fans. It was time to celebrate.

Coach Redding shares the Big Ten trophy with his players.

8

Doorstep

With our second-chance victory over Hastings, our school had won only its second Big Ten football championship ever. Bulldog football had been down for so long that the last six seasons had yielded only eleven victories.

Yet, even with that impressive victory and conference championship, the best our school could do in the final *Omaha World-Herald* statewide ranking was climb to sixth place behind five Lincoln and Omaha schools. Our fans were outraged. They were convinced there was an "out-state" prejudice against us by the metro-area paper.

I wasn't so sure. With our regular-season losses to Hastings and Grand Island, let alone our two ties, I was satisfied with being in the top ten.

After reading the *World-Herald*'s accompanying articles, I leaned back on our sofa and reflected over all that happened in three short months.

In Coach Redding's first year, he promised the school board and us players we would win more games than we lost. He had more than delivered with a 6–2–2 season and a coveted Big Ten championship.

The two teams we had tied each finished with undefeated seasons. Sidney was chosen as Nebraska's Class B champion and Sterling won Colorado's Class A championship. Coach Redding had been correct. They were two fine teams, and our record was even better than it appeared.

Coach Redding was deservedly a hero. He was the focus of several radio and TV interviews, and many articles were written touting his turnaround abilities. Larry and Pete were equally justified in being singled out as making the largest contributions to the team.

I was also impressed by the seniors as a group. Loyal to Coach Easter and more set in their ways than our class, they had made a great adjustment to Coach Redding's methods. I was surprised by the way they sucked it up.

Other than me, the starting offensive line was all seniors. The one I came to know best was left-tackle Gary Scheet. Playing next to him all season allowed me to see a determined, mature athlete in action.

I had never before "gotten" football, but Gary helped me see the subtleties and small but important decisions involved in every play and series. Gary's judgment was superlative, and it helped he was a bit of a moose, too, as no one got his measure. I also learned from him how to have fun at football, as when we would bury an opposing player into other players or into the ground.

"Fun" was definitely not a description that would characterize Coach Redding's practices. Yet the seniors found small opportunities to create some laughter, even at a cost. Byron was the master at finding those rare moments, but he always paid a price for his transgressions.

The most humorous episode of the season, though, involved our classmate Allan Whitesel. He gave us one of those memorable insider-stories that became part of our team's lore.

Allan was a quick, scrappy kid. His relentless effort so impressed Coach Redding, Allan was often used for kickoff and punt returns early in the season.

The protocol for a return was to have Allan tell us whether he was going to run to our left or right. Based on his choice, the rest of us would form a wall of blockers for him on the side he designated.

Sometimes Allan would run to the side he called out, but as often as not, we would be positioning ourselves on the designated-return side of the field only to watch Allan running to the other side and getting creamed.

At first we thought it was an aberration, but it happened over and over again. His massacres were comical in their totality, much as we tried not to laugh at him. The defenders, meanwhile, could not believe their good fortune at having no blockers between them and the ball carrier, and they poured into him with abandon.

After a game in which we experienced another such incident, we learned while taking our showers Allan also kept failing his driver's license test. Someone asked him what part of the test he was failing, and he said it was his making improper turns after the tester's instructions to turn left or right.

Ah-hah. We had the answer to Allan's dilemma on the football field: he had dyslexia. He could not tell left from right.

We suggested he tape the letters L and R on his hands for his next driver's license test, and sure enough, he passed. To see if we could get the same type of success at football, we had him call out "Our bench" or "Their bench" to indicate his intended direction for the kick returns.

Using that suggestion, he finally was able to gain some yards behind our protection and avoid getting wiped out.

The mystery surrounding Allan had been solved, but we never let him forget it.

●　●　●

As underclassmen, our final task to button up the season was to choose a team captain for the following year. Pete and Larry were chosen to lead our team for our senior year, and deservedly so. Both shone defensively, with Pete controlling the middle of the field and Larry protecting against anything deep.

They also dominated the individual offensive statistics chart for the year. Larry and Pete had been first and second in rushing, and Larry stood alone in total offense at almost 1,800 yards. In the Big Ten title game alone, Larry gained ninety yards in kickoff returns to go along with his 170 rushing yards on fourteen carries for a 12.1 yards-per-carry average. Although Larry had one more touchdown

Pete and Larry are voted in by the players as next year's co-captains.

than Pete for the year, Pete edged out Larry for the scoring lead with PAT's included, since Pete most often was the ballcarrier on our point-after attempts.

Although the lion's share of starters was graduating, our future still looked bright, given that rare offensive combination Larry and Pete afforded us.

Throughout the season I gained more and more respect for Larry. He was unflappable, confident of his abilities, and comfortable with the expectations that preceded him. He was always "on," functioning at the highest performance level.

I was rarely shocked by the spectacular things Larry did. Still, the unique essence of his athleticism intrigued me, as I couldn't put my finger on what separated him from the rest of us.

As for Pete, I admired how he had taken his game and reputation to a new level. He came alive under Coach Redding, impressing everyone with his talent. Football was the perfect sport and outlet for Pete.

Contrast Pete's junior year with his earlier athletic shortfalls, and the only answer for his transformation was Coach Redding. Pete's pent-up emotions and energies became channeled into fire-hose intensity for football. Something in Coach Redding's rhetoric, work ethic, communication style, and demand for personal excellence so inspired Pete, it made him into a new person.

He had gone from being an afterthought to a top statewide college prospect in just a few short months, with the promise of more to come. His emergence as a star of our team had been remarkable.

With Larry and a rejuvenated Pete providing the spark, I figured we had a good start toward having a successful team for our senior year. But I did worry that our interior offensive line was going to be small and untested.

My classmates who would likely fill the graduating seniors' positions were barely in the 140-pound range. Tough and well intentioned, maybe, but just not big enough. Plus, last season's Grand Island game exposed a significant defensive-line weakness up the middle, which I had no idea how we would shore up. All I knew was, based on my performance in that game, I was not the answer.

Coach Redding would have to solve that problem, as he had most other problems. The "nose-guard defense" aside, Coach had been proven correct on all of his strategies.

As for his assistants, Coach Ray Best worked with the linemen, so I came to be more familiar with him. He had Coach Redding's confidence and our respect, and although Coach Redding overshadowed everyone, Coach Best held his own.

Coach Folsom, on the other hand, was still a mystery to me. He worked with the backs, so I didn't interact with him at all. Larry didn't have much to say about him, either. I hoped during basketball season, when he could come out from under Coach Redding's dominating personality, he would develop a good relationship with us.

Not that I had any kind of close rapport with Coach Redding. Yet I did admire him in a confusing way.

I had liked coaches before Coach Redding, and I had disliked coaches before him. But before Coach Redding, I had never let a coach

Coach George "Crump" Redding

get inside my protective wall that dealt with the amount of effort I chose to exert at any one time, my self-assessment of my performance, and my self-esteem. What was even more mystifying was I had not *let* him in—he had crashed down my barricade with his presumptive assumption that we were all in his care to be the best we could be, individually and collectively.

It didn't matter to Coach Redding if we liked that or not. We had a choice, and if we chose to wear his football uniforms, then we played the game by his rules, not ours.

● ● ●

Late in the season, Allan and I had talked about this aspect of our relationship with Coach Redding while walking home one night after practice. Allan had asked, "What is it about Coach that has us respect him and accept him for who he is?"

I answered, "Darned if I know. Maybe it has something to do with his wanting only what's best for the team. He treats everyone the same and accepts only our top effort. I've tuned out other coaches for criticizing me, but not him.

"What's your opinion?"

Allan thought a while, then offered, "He strips you bare, takes away all of your excuses, and then demands and gets more than you knew you had available to give. But whatever he says is never personal, so it's not embarrassing. Right?"

"I don't know how he does it, but you're right. If he gets angry, it's not at *us*, it's at what we've done or not done. And it's the same for every one of us, and it's the same every moment we're on the field."

For whatever reasons, all of us on the team had completely bought into Coach Redding. And although I still couldn't say I liked football, it now made sense to me. I could finally relate to the teamwork required to fulfill his various offensive and defensive strategies.

I figured I'd let him worry about any problems facing us for the following year. Besides, I needed to shift my attention to more important things.

I had to start getting mentally prepared to jump into basketball season. Ever since I fell in love with sports in the fifth grade, ever since we had signed the Pledge as freshmen, the heralded basketball season I had dreamed about was about to start.

This would be our moment.

"State by '63!" was at hand.

9

Now What?

Coach, Coach,
Open the door.
Let our Bulldogs
On the floor!

Coach, Coach,
Open the door.
Let our Bulldogs
On the floor!

It was the first home basketball game of our race to the state championship. Coach Folsom was giving us our final pregame instructions, but who could hear him?

The student section of the bleachers was right above our locker room. Fueled by Pep Band, Pep Club, and Letterman's Club members, the mind-numbing, repetitive chant would continue until we reappeared up the steps onto the court. Our locker room was being crushed under the foot-stomping and drum-beating rhythms.

I reflected on our transition from football to basketball. It had been a rocky road from the start between us players and Coach Folsom. At issue was a clash of wills. Being an effective coach involves many variables, and the personalities of the coach and his team need to match up in a productive way for an optimum result.

In Coach Redding's case, his successful entry as the school's new football coach, even though the previous coach was well liked, was facilitated by his strong persona and the team's historically poor record. There had been no preexisting cohesive team personality with which to contend, so he was able to create a group mentality loyal to him. Plus, it didn't hurt it was clear from the get-go he knew more about football than any of us did.

Our new basketball coach didn't have any of those advantages. Coach Folsom ran headfirst into a successful, well-honed, like-minded, and self-motivated core group of players who were fiercely loyal to one another.

We also missed Coach Smith's more aggressive style. And all of us thought we—or, at the very least, Coach Smith—knew more about basketball than Coach Folsom did.

The relentless noise from above brought me back to the moment.

1961–1962 varsity basketball team, *from left to right:* Darrel Gale, Larry Wachholtz, Roy Wagner, Jim States, Bill Stephenson, Bob Thomas,

It was exhilarating to play in front of a rabidly partisan crowd. North Platte fans supported all of our teams in every sport, but being at arms' length with their spirit inside a gym was breathtaking.

I caught the tail end of Coach Folsom's speech. "Our starting lineup will be States, Stephenson, Wachholtz, Gale, and Thomas."

He had gotten off on the wrong foot with the five of us. He ultimately settled on the obvious starting lineup inherited from the previous season, but in our opinion he had wasted a lot of valuable time by trying various lineup combinations. He never engaged with us as a special entity.

As a result, we never shared our Pledge with him. He knew of our desire to go to state but did not know the source of our dream or how young we were when we had committed to it.

Once again, we were a team not fully integrated with our coach.

Denny Nelson, Jim Huffman, Jack Edwards, Gene Jones, Galen Skinner, and Bob Reuter

And after surrendering by demand to Coach Redding with positive results, it never occurred to me that we might be too immature to willingly do the same for Coach Folsom for the betterment of the team.

"Let's go!"

We might not have had a tight rapport with him, but we did with each other. We wanted to get this season under way. Released by him, we bounded down the hall, turned right, and took the stairs two at a time up to court level. At that moment, the thrilling possibility of a dominating victory was the only thought running through our psyched-up minds.

Jim called us together on the court before we positioned ourselves for the opening tip. Bent over, hands on my knees, I studied the number 32 on his jersey as he shared his passion for the task ahead. "All right, here we go. This is the season we've been waiting for. Nobody can take what's ours. Give it everything you've got, all the way."

So motivated, we started out the season with solid victories over Sidney and Lincoln Northeast before facing our coach's former team, Ogallala.

Ogallala had two advantages going for them. First, they were determined to show up the coach they felt had deserted them. Second, Larry was not able to play. He had to take some time off to let a nagging football-induced knee injury heal. Given those benefits in their favor, they played us tough before falling in the final moments.

We got away without Larry against Ogallala but weren't so lucky against Hastings. It was our last game before the Christmas holiday. Against three players who averaged a full five inches over our front line, we got off to a bad start and never recovered. They soundly trounced us, 52–35.

It wasn't just Larry's absence that did us in. When I went over to his home after the game to wind down, he angrily got right to the point.

"You guys were intimidated by their size. I've never seen that happen before. They aren't going to be the only team we face this year that will be taller than us, so you big guys had better learn to handle it."

As usual, he was right.

The next day, Jim and I talked about Larry's criticism. He agreed with Larry.

Elaborating, he noted, "On defense, we needed to keep them from getting under the basket all the time. We also needed to block out for rebounds better. On offense, we just tightened up. If we had been moving at our normal speed, their height wouldn't have mattered."

We used the days off to good advantage and regrouped. With both Larry and our team's self-confidence healed, Alliance became our first victim of the new year. We were back on track, mentally and physically.

The second game after the holidays was one to remember. We put together our best basketball game ever against a strong Scottsbluff team. Each school's group of players genuinely liked and respected each other. No matter what the sport, a game between our two teams could be counted upon to light it up.

The game was expected to be close, and it was for a while. But with six minutes left to go, we switched into a special gear. Our runaway score of 80–51 marked the first time in the history of our schools' rivalry a team had reached 80 points.

Our balanced scoring was representative of our unique teamwork. Larry and Jim Huffman led us with 17 points. Huffman had been given a starting nod for the first time and had made the best of it. I was next with 16, Jim States had 15, and Darrel contributed 8.

It was one of those special "in the zone" nights that had been foretold the year before in the late-season McCook game. It was as if the opposition had no choice but to capitulate.

From that game on, we were at full strength and ran off a 9–1 record to close out the regular season at 14–2, the best record in our school's history.

Our only blemish in the last ten-game string was against Grand Island. That loss was highly beneficial, however, as it released a growing self-expectation pressure from within our team.

As desirous of success as we were, we were equally unprepared to handle it. As the victory count increased, the students and townspeople became progressively more passionate for the next triumph.

We, on the other hand, became grumpy. We argued with the

cheerleaders about their using us for their school-spirit purposes. We complained about everything. The joy had disappeared. We wanted to retreat into a cocoon and play only for ourselves.

The loss to Grand Island slapped us in the face and reset our perceptions. We woke up to the realization our fans were on our side, not against us. They were only enjoying what we were creating. We refocused on our team goals and finished out the regular season in high gear and with the proper attitude.

With a perfect West division record, we easily took that sub-championship. Ahead of us was our second Big Ten conference opportunity in just a few months. The basketball title game would be immediately followed by our district-qualifying tournament to move on to the state tournament.

Normally we would have felt getting to the state tournament was our singular priority, but all of a sudden we wanted it all. The unexpected thrill of the football season's championship over Hastings whetted our appetite for the Big Ten conference basketball title. Most of all, though, we fervently believed it was our year. We had no doubt we could handle any challenge before us.

The conference title game would be a great test of our state-championship aspirations. Our foe was the Fremont Tigers—the defending state basketball champs.

One night during the week leading up to the game, Larry and I discussed our challenge ahead. I told him, "They're a terrific team. They've won all of their conference games, just like we did. And they've won the same number of games overall as we have."

Larry added, "What impresses me most is they have the same lineup that won the state championship last year. They returned all of their starters. They know how to win the big ones."

"This will be a perfect checkpoint for us," I concluded. "We'll find out if we have the team we think we do."

On game day, a driving snowstorm caused the school administration to cancel the school bus for the trip to Fremont. We had to split up into the coaches' cars to inch our way there. The trip took hours, and the car I was in with the rest of the starters had a temperamental heater. One minute we were cooking and the next, freezing. I was grateful when we finally made it to Fremont's gym.

During "warm-ups"—thinking of that term made me laugh because I was still freezing my ass off—the public announcer asked the local Fremont supporters "to squeeze it in." Their fans good-naturedly complied so at least two dozen half-frozen North Platte supporters left standing outside in the snowstorm could edge their hind ends into the crowded bleachers. That made a few hundred North Platte people who toughed it out to get there. I couldn't believe so many made such an effort.

We started the game hitting on all cylinders and led at the end of the first quarter, 23–12. Everyone on both teams took it up a notch for the second quarter, but our eleven-point margin was still maintained at halftime, 34–23.

Without realizing I was that spent and tired, I fell asleep from exhaustion during the halftime break. But I rushed out rejuvenated and fully committed for the second half, and everyone else seemed to have made the same intense rededication.

Regardless, the strong will of the Fremont players and their stifling full-court press steadily pulled them back into the game. With only a few seconds left in the game, they tied the score.

Darrel quickly took the ball out of bounds, threw it to Larry, who rifled a toss to Jim States. As a natural left-hander, he was moving down the court on the left as I filled the lane to the right. The one person defending us was 6' 5" Ed Rainey.

As Rainey moved to cover States with the clock running down, he also expertly blocked the passing lane to me and forced Jim to move a little wider than he intended. The result was all Jim could do was fling up an awkward shot that ricocheted hard off the backboard and rattled around and around the rim.

The shot finally eased its way into the net, with resulting pandemonium from the North Platte faithful. Our fans stormed the court and surrounded us as we all circled around, hugging each other and bouncing up and down. We had played the game of our lives.

It felt great to pass this formidable test. We were more certain than ever we were a team of destiny.

Soaking it all in while taking our showers, we basked in the glory of winning a second Big Ten championship in the same year for the first time in our school's history. We had also taken another giant step toward our goal as being the best in the state.

Just as in the preceding football season when we were Big Ten champs, however, the Lincoln and Omaha weekend papers ranked us only at sixth place behind five Lincoln and Omaha schools, even though we had the highest number of victories in the state at fifteen.

We didn't care. Our time would soon come.

The following week, we were off to McCook for the district tournament to take the next step in our destiny and fulfillment of our Pledge. The state's Class A basketball champion would be determined by gathering the eight district champions to play in a winner-takes-all tournament at the university field house in Lincoln.

We fully expected to be that champion. All we had to do was clear the easy district hurdle, and off we would go to state.

Entering the district tournament only a few days after returning home from Fremont, our first game was against McCook. Just a few weeks before, we had annihilated them, 86–37. This time, however, we were dealing with a mental letdown after the Fremont game, and our starting five had severe head colds from the wintry trip to and from Fremont.

Combined with a valiant effort from McCook, the game was tight much of the way, although we eventually prevailed, 55–41.

One evening later, our district title game was against Holdrege. A much smaller school, we had conquered them decisively, 67–49, in the last game of our regular season.

We wanted this game badly, so we could "get to state."

As the game got under way, not much was working. It felt as if we were operating in quicksand. The reason was Holdrege had a great game plan to defend us. We would take the ball out of bounds and move it quickly up court, like always. Or we would get a defensive rebound and race toward our basket in our patented fast break. But everywhere we went, the Holdrege defenders were there ahead of us, in our way. It seemed no sooner did we make a move to the basket than Holdrege would intercept a pass, and back we would go on defense.

Despite their defensive mastery, we ended the first half ahead, 32–30. I was confused by their surprising effectiveness, but I wasn't worried. I knew we would crush them in the second half with our talented ballplayers and teamwork born of years of playing with one another on the driveways of North Platte.

During his halftime talk, Coach Folsom opined Holdrege's Coach Merle Bauer apparently used their free week, while we were playing Fremont for the conference title, to prepare for this game. He said they were using a collapsing zone and not taking any of our feints, thereby intercepting our usual blind passes to one another. That's why it had seemed like they knew exactly what we were going to do.

An alarm bell went off in my head. Could we be that easy to defend? OK, so that was the problem. What should we do about it? What did Coach Folsom want us to do about it?

"Play harder out there, boys! Make your passes more crisply and move the ball around from side to side. Larry, keep moving the ball around until you find an opening."

Larry had a look on his face like he thought that's what he had been doing. The problem was in finding an opening. I glanced at Jim. He was staring down at his shoes with the same look. Darrel glanced at me. I agreed with their silent concern.

I finally decided there was no good reason for me to complain. I didn't have a better idea. I didn't know what would solve their constant interceptions of our passes. We were so accustomed to playing with one another, we constantly made blind passes to each other, knowing full well everyone's next move. But now Holdrege seemed to know the same thing.

I did know I could play harder. I could do that. Anyway, I was sure we would somehow break away from them.

But as the second half got under way, the opposite happened—on both offense and defense.

They changed their defense to a "box and one" four-man zone around the basket with one player assigned exclusively to guard Larry. While we were not a one-man offense, Holdrege's Coach Bauer had figured out another way to interrupt our flow and our natural way of

Coach Joe Folsom and trainer Max Byersdorf watch the action.

playing. With Larry restricted from initiating plays, our key source of generating scoring opportunities was shut down.

At the same time, Holdrege forward Stan Schlachter was going on a tear. We held him to one point just two weeks earlier, but now he was ripping us apart. He was knocking down everything he threw at the basket.

Before we knew it, we had been outscored in the third quarter 23–7 and were now down fourteen points. We were in a deep hole.

Looking at each other in our huddle around Coach Folsom before the start of the fourth quarter, I was gratified to see resolve in everyone's eyes. No fear, no more assumed confidence—just determination.

The game turned into a blur of effort beyond anything we had ever exerted. Everything we had ever wanted was on the line.

"Play harder!"

"Hustle back!"

"Screen!"

"Block out. Get that rebound."

"Loose ball!"

"Let's go!"

"Don't foul!"

In the midst of our frenzy, a buzzer sounded. The game was over?

It couldn't be! Wasn't there another quarter left? This couldn't be it.

My God, we lost? Lost to Holdrege? Holdrege, for chrissakes? We're not going to state? We actually lost this game? I could not comprehend it. I could not believe it.

States was still in motion. He was not ready to stop playing. Larry would not leave the floor.

No one would look at the Holdrege players rejoicing and laughing, hugging their coach. We wanted more. We needed more. It couldn't possibly be over.

It was a hollow feeling—as if my body was suspended in air, bracing for a hurtful plunge to earth.

We reluctantly moved to the locker room and sat motionless on the benches. Unable to take off our uniforms and thereby acknowledge the finality of the game, our season, and our dream, we tried to make some sense of it.

Bill, clearly upset, blurted out, "We were just outplayed and outcoached. We underestimated them."

Jim disagreed. "I think we were affected by the Fremont win and our being sick, but I believe we were ready to play. Their coach just had us scouted perfectly."

Jim Huffman observed, "Their defensive sets were genius. They took us out of our game, for sure."

Darrel added, "And who expected that out of Schlachter? He must have had half their points tonight."

I contributed, "I feel so sorry for you seniors. This was the year we had been looking for, and it's all over. We let you down."

Larry summed it up best. "I'm pissed. We let *ourselves* down. We got worried too late. We always assumed we would figure it out, but we didn't. This hurts more than I could ever have imagined."

Peeling off his jersey, he captured our mood, "I hate losing. God, I hate losing."

Whether we were caught looking ahead, still emotionally spent from the Fremont game, simply outcoached and outplayed by Holdrege, or taken down by a great individual scoring effort by Schlachter, we found ourselves on a long bus ride home with the bitter taste of a

62–54 loss in our mouths and an emptiness in our chests.

The past week had contained both our most thrilling, uplifting victory against mighty Fremont and our most crushing, heartrending defeat at the hands of lowly Holdrege. The magnitudes of the high and low further intensified the pain of the upset.

With all we had accomplished throughout the year, for all the records we had set, for all our justifiable expectations, we were left with nothing. Fate had not won this game for us, after all.

I knew then and there we would each remember "the Holdrege game" with the same ache in our hearts for the rest of our lives. We were devastated. We had literally thrown away our second and best chance at honoring our pledge. We knew intuitively this was the team to fulfill the Pledge, and we had squandered our opportunity.

Our passionate "State by '63!" declaration, which had always seemed inevitable and so close at hand, now looked far, far away and very unlikely. Our self-perceptions were shattered. We were completely unprepared psychologically to live with our failure. Had not "State By '63!" been our fate-blessed destiny?

● ● ●

The following Monday morning, as I walked into the school building, all I could think was, Now what? Really—now what?

The last person in the world I wanted to see was Coach Redding. I was in grave emotional distress, yet I knew there was no way he would be sympathetic.

It was if he had been waiting for me. I shuddered throughout my whole body as I saw him striding toward me.

"Thomas! You turds had no business losing that game. That was horseshit. Why couldn't you figure out what was happening? It was as obvious as the shirt on your back."

"Yes, sir." But the fact was we didn't figure it out.

"You had a team that could have gone all the way, and you didn't even get in the door. That's criminal."

"Yes, sir, I know." And that, I truly did know . . .

10

Road Trip

Crump Redding was also the school's head track coach, which gave him the chance to use the facilities as spring training for football. Those who weren't actively engaged in preparing for track meets worked out with weights and wind sprints.

Track season played out uneventfully, though several of us qualified for the state track championships. Instead of taking a team bus to the university in Lincoln, we split up to ride in the coaches' cars.

I was assigned, along with Larry, Marv, and a couple of others, to be in Coach Redding's car. From the moment we left the school grounds, he was in a talkative mood.

"You know how I came to be coaching in North Platte? The school board members decided they were tired of losing at football. They fired Easter and then realized they didn't know how to find the coach they were looking for. That's when the young attorney Harold Kay, who's president of the school board, made a suggestion to the board they should contact the college-football head coaches in neighboring states to see who the top high-school coaches in their state were.

"They knew not to contact the University of Nebraska coaching staff, because they were as miserable as what you had here in North Platte. That was before the university hired Bob Devaney this year from Wyoming. I tell you, he is a good one.

"So, Otto Oakes, your superintendent of schools, called Jack Mitchell at Kansas University. Mitchell told Oakes the guy who routinely sent him the best players—most well trained in football fundamentals—was me. I know, because Jack called me right afterwards. Then, sure enough, Oakes called my school in Larned to get permission to talk to me. Oakes phoned me to come visit North Platte.

"The whole board met with me at the Pawnee Hotel. They wanted me to make a formal presentation. I told them there was no reason a school the size of North Platte should lose as many games every year as it did. North Platte should always win more than it loses.

"But I also told them it wasn't going to happen if their players were coddled. You had to treat them like men and light a fire under them. If the board wanted a nice coach who was friendly with the players, they didn't want me. If they wanted a tough sonuvabitch who would kick the boys' asses six ways from Sunday until they learned how to play football the right way, then I was the one they wanted."

Looking around the car at each of us for emphasis, he added, "I guess that's what they wanted, and that's what I'm giving them."

He continued, "Almost a year ago, Oakes and I sealed the deal. That day, after we finished, I walked outdoors to visit my new office, and to my surprise almost all of my new players were out there on the varsity field. You scaredycats looked like you were afraid I was going to kick you off."

"We were, Coach. We had no idea who you were," Larry confirmed. Changing the subject, he asked, "I understand why the school board would have wanted you, but why did you decide to come to North Platte?"

"That's a long story," Coach Redding began.

"Before I was born, my future dad, A. P. Redding, was a wildcatter in the oil fields of Oklahoma—a tough job and a tough guy if ever there was one. At some point, he fell for a girl, and she fell for him. Trouble was, she had a boyfriend or fiancé or something, who her parents liked and wanted her to marry.

"One night, A. P. and the girl snuck off to a dance. The boyfriend heard about that, and so he and his buddies went over to catch A.P. leaving the dance. They jumped him to beat him up and teach him a lesson.

"Wrong guy to mess with. The boyfriend pulled a knife on A.P., but he was the one that ended up dead. A. P. was arrested for murder.

"The parents of both the girl and the dead boyfriend plus half the town wanted A. P. hanged. The other half said the dead boyfriend got what was coming to him. The only guy whose opinion mattered, though, was the town judge. He ended up settling the case and released A. P. to his freedom. Not long thereafter A. P. and the girl married.

"I was their firstborn son, and in lasting appreciation they named me after Judge George Crump. My birth certificate reads George Crump Redding, though most people nowadays just call me 'Crump.'

"Anyway, Dad was still a wildcatter and kept moving from oil field to oil field, always chasing that next big strike. I went to eleven different grade schools and three different high schools. Seemed like every time we moved, I'd have to fight all the boys in the town so a new pecking order was established. I learned I liked being on top of the totem pole, but even so, I decided if I ever had a family, I'd never subject them to that kind of nomadic life.

"Thinking I was pretty tough, I figured I was ready for the war, so I joined the Army Air Force and went overseas. There's some stories there, boys.

"But before I shipped out, I attended a USO dance in Paterson, New Jersey. A girl had invited me to go, and so I did. But by the time the dance event was finished, I had hit it off with her friend Ruth.

"There wasn't much time, and the USO had rules against fraternization, but I promised Ruth I would return and marry her. I did. I came back after the war as promised, and we got married.

"I brought Ruth to Oklahoma and started wildcatting just like my dad to make some money. It was so tough on our marriage, I quit and went to college on the GI Bill to learn a career.

"Most people assume I lost my eye during the war. No, I lost it about ten years ago in a volleyball game, where some idiot phys-ed student poked his finger in my eye.

"Say, that reminds me. Remember the day I first met you I was wearing an eye patch? I had dropped my favorite glass eye and broke it. My backup was giving me fits, so I had to settle for wearing the eye patch when I met with Mr. Oakes and the school board."

I thought it had been a smart move, even if accidental. As menacing as he looked to us, he had to look like something pretty special to the school board—someone who would instill needed discipline in his new charges.

Coach Redding continued. "I'd better get back to my story. After I went to college, Ruth and I started a family, and I started coaching. We moved to Kansas, and at my first coaching job in Grenola, they had only seventeen boys in the whole school. But I still played them at a full eleven-man team schedule rather than a six- or eight-man schedule.

"After Grenola, I went to a bigger school in Clearwater for four years, and then on to Larned. Jack Mitchell, who was then head coach at Wichita State, recommended me for the Larned job, too. I stayed there for seven years, bringing them seven winning seasons and a state championship.

"That state championship was something. Our town numbered only five-thousand people, and we beat schools from Wichita and the college towns to take the title. No one thought something like that could happen. We shocked the whole state.

"As my oldest, Clark, was ready to start high school, I knew then was the time to move. I wanted to move someplace where I could stay until all six of my kids had graduated from the same high school.

"I get offers from colleges every year, but those college jobs are too unstable. Staying in one place is more important to me. Besides, North Platte looked very similar to the situation I found in Larned. I like the underdog position for the surprise element and figured we could sneak up on a few teams before they knew what hit them, since everyone was so used to mopping the floor with you boys.

"I also knew you couldn't be as bad as your football record. I knew I could win a few games a year just on improved fundamentals. And I knew with your school enrollment, I had to be able to find enough boys to field a decent team.

"I'm here in North Platte now, and I intend to stay until Clark, Robert, Doris, David, and the twins—Dan and Denise—all graduate from high school."

He wasn't kidding. It *had* been a long story. We had learned a lot about Coach Redding on the trip to Lincoln.

● ● ●

With the state track meet completed, we wondered what the topic would be on the way home. Surprisingly, though, he was quiet. He looked tired.

Bored, we boys decided to pass the time by telling each other our most embarrassing moment. Marv said, "Larry, you thought of it. You go first!"

Larry, riding shotgun, groaned but started us off on our road game. "The problem is, there are so many, I don't know where to start. Hey, I know! I can tell you one that involves Bob, too."

"That's cheating!" I called out to everyone. "Don't listen to him."

Ignoring me, Larry began. "Last summer Bob calls me from the ranch he's working at to see if I can come up for the weekend. He says two girls from Iowa are staying there for a week on a FHA-exchange program. They had agreed to a Saturday-night moonlight horseback ride, so can I come help him out on a double date? Being the nice guy I am, I say 'Sure.'"

I interjected, "One of the cowboys had suggested I ask them out for the ride, so I did. But when they both said yes, I got scared. I didn't know what to do."

"Hey!" Larry said, looking back at me, grinning. "This is my story to tell. Anyway, I drive up there to spend Saturday night with Bob. For the big moonlight ride, we get all cleaned up, saddle up four horses, walk them to the main house to pick up the girls, and ride off into the night.

"It's a beautiful evening. The moon and stars are shining, the girls are cute, and everything is perfect.

"Bob seems like he knows where to go, so we end up where there are two blowouts close to each other up in the hills. The wind had created two big erosions in the sand—perfect for each of us couples.

"We were ready for some romance in case the girls were game, and sure enough, they were. We unsaddled the horses and put the saddles on the ground. We tied each horse's reins to a saddle horn so the horses would stay put, and we took the saddle blankets with us into the deep blowouts."

I was shaking my head. I knew what was coming.

"Before too long, the girl with Bob screams bloody murder. The girl I'm with starts to scream, too, so I jump up to look around. What I see almost scares the crap out of me.

"All around the perimeter of our blowout are more than a dozen pairs of eyes glowing in the moonlight, glaring down at us! All I can think about are *coyotes*. One or two coyotes wouldn't be a big problem, but a whole pack of them could be huge trouble. We had nothing to defend ourselves.

"I'm mentally running through our survival options when my eyes start to adjust to the situation, and I see what's really going on. The menacing eyes belonged to cattle! That's all they were—just cattle!"

Everyone burst out laughing.

Larry picked up the story again. "Jeez! Unbelievable! I guess they had heard the goings-on and had decided to assemble themselves around the rims of both blowouts as if having reserved seating for best viewing.

"On one hand I'm relieved they aren't coyotes, but on the other hand I'm frustrated at these stupid cows trampling all over the romantic mood we had established.

"The four of us climb out of the blowouts. Standing right in the middle of a whole herd of cows, we look at each other like, 'Are you kidding me?'

"We have a few nervous laughs and then reluctantly agree we should head back home. We push through the cattle and walk over to the horses.

"Horses? What horses? We've got saddles scattered all around, but no horses! They disappeared. I guess they got spooked from the screaming and slipped our tie-ups."

The guys in the car were enjoying this story way too much. They were grinning wider and wider with each new revelation. They knew what Larry and I would have to do.

Larry rewarded their anticipation. "Bob and I each hoist a saddle on our shoulders, and we all head back on the long, embarrassing walk to the ranch complex. After depositing the girls safe and sound where they were staying, we find our missing horses in the barn, eating hay like nothing had happened.

"We saddle up again and go back into the hills to retrieve the other two saddles. After returning to the barn and brushing down all four horses, we finally get to bed, our damaged self-images still somewhat intact."

"That is, until breakfast," I interjected.

Larry hooted. "The girls told everybody everything! We city slickers were the laughingstocks of the whole ranch, and there was nothing we could do but take it."

The guys were laughing hard.

"That's a good one, Larry!"

"You guys are stumblebums!"

"You could screw up a wet dream."

Even Coach Redding had a smile on his face.

"OK, Bob, it's your turn," Marv directed.

"That's not fair! That one was about me, too. Larry went home on Sunday, but I had to listen to that baloney for the rest of the summer. And besides, as usual with me and girls, nothing happened anyway."

Larry countered, "Maybe, but you were hoping."

Yes, I suppose I had been hoping. And maybe I could get back at Larry for telling that story. "OK, I'll go next. The least I can do is return the favor to Larry and tell one that involves him.

"After we lost the district basketball game to Holdrege, a trip was arranged for us to go to Lincoln to watch the state tournament. We were told it would inspire us to make it to state on our own our senior year.

"A bunch of our girlfriends started talking about organizing their own trip to Lincoln, so they could meet up with us. We planned a nice rendezvous at the hotel where we would be staying, but then their trip fell apart. They were pretty disappointed.

"But I got to thinking. I had met this girl from Wahoo, just a few miles from Lincoln, at the state music clinic last year in Fremont, and we had written each other a few times. I check with her, and sure enough, she agrees to come to Lincoln to see me again. She also says her best friend would like to meet Larry. I ask Larry, and he says OK."

Larry grimaced in anticipation of the rest of the story. "Remember, this was Bob's idea."

Undaunted, I continued. "So the two girls from Wahoo meet us as planned in the hotel lobby. We go through our introductions and start heading out of the hotel to find a place to have lunch. We almost get to the front door when all of a sudden we hear two familiar female voices excitedly call out from the registration area. 'Larry!' 'Bob!'"

Coach Redding interrupted, "Hey, here's the turnoff to Hastings. They are going to have a great team again next year."

Either our stories reenergized him, or he wanted to protect Larry and me from ourselves in our storytelling. In any event, he started in again, suddenly as talkative as on our ride to Lincoln.

"You know, I've been really impressed with the school spirit in North Platte, as well as the spirit around the whole town. I was amazed when di Natalie got all the businesses and residents to answer every phone call with 'Beat Hastings!' That was really something. That's all I heard for a week!"

As Coach paused for a moment, Marv leaned over to me in the backseat and whispered, "Bob, finish your story. What happened?"

"Heck, no. No more embarrassing moments." I knew Larry and I had been saved. "Besides, Coach is on a roll."

Sure enough, Coach Redding continued. "You boys may not know this, but when I got to North Platte, one of the first things I did was to have the cheerleaders and Pep Club officers over to our home. I've always done that wherever I've coached, every year. Ruth made them a nice picnic, and I told them how important they were to getting the school spirit soaring. I told them my boys will play a lot harder if their chests are pumped up with pride in representing their school.

"The girls got all excited and told me they wanted to put me and you boys up on the stage during pep rallies to help them, and I said, 'No way! My boys have their stage performances during the games. Those pep rallies are *your* responsibility. Let's see what you can do with them. Let's see you get the students and teachers involved instead.' And darned if they didn't do even better than I had hoped for. Those pep rallies have been spectacular."

I agreed with his assessment, but was surprised to hear he was the stimulus for those new rallies.

The pep rallies had become highly entertaining mini-stage productions. Individual Pep Club members were assigned on a rotating basis to be in charge of organizing each weekly rally. They enlisted the services of other students as well as teachers to help write scripts and act out parts.

For one skit, Herb Burch, who was also the school annual's photographer, helped create a Shakespearean knockoff where three witches boiled up a winning brew. Another skit, a takeoff on the movie *South Pacific*, had teachers and students alike dancing around the stage in grass skirts and other Polynesian-themed garb.

The memorable assemblies were talked about for days, sometimes well past the conversations about the games themselves. Everyone wondered what could or would be done to top the previous one.

Coach Redding added, "Another thing you may not know or realize is why there are only boys' sports here in North Platte. Never thought about it, right? That's not the case in most other places—only here in Nebraska at the Class A level. Even all of the lower class levels in the state have girls' sports.

"I asked why and was told some cockamamie story about the Class A schools deciding to eliminate girls' sports way back in the early thirties based on Eleanor Roosevelt making a statement that sports were unbecoming to ladies. Even if true, and I bet it's not, times have changed.

"You guys should appreciate all the time these girls give to support your sports programs. It's time they would otherwise be spending on their own activities."

That made me feel bad all over again about the events surrounding the Grand Island game during the recent basketball season. Crap! Remembering it, I cringed, just like I did with my embarrassing moments.

After our season had started with multiple wins, we ballplayers began to feel the pressure to continue our success. We took it out on the cheerleaders by accusing them of undermining us by getting everyone excessively enthused about our success. Their tears and disappointment in us were no match for our stubbornness and misguided self-pity as we kept on ranting. Once we lost to Grand Island, though, the pressure escaped and we were back in our right minds as if it never happened. The girls thankfully forgave us and we moved on.

Coach Redding was still talking. "School spirit here in North Platte is as good or better than any place I've ever seen, but it takes work. And sacrifice. Those girls who make this all happen could play on my team anytime."

I was surprised at how strongly he felt about the girls' efforts and contributions. It provided me with a characteristic of his personality I would never have thought was there. I was learning there was a lot more to this man than what was on the surface.

11

V-I-C-T-O-R-Y

Late Spring, 1962

Miss Helen Shields, Pep Club sponsor, climbed up the stairs to the senior-high auditorium stage. Presiding over the annual varsity-cheerleader tryout and selection, she addressed the full-capacity crowd.

"Boys and girls, this is a very important day for these young ladies who have qualified to win your vote. Group participation is contagious, and it's the role of your cheerleaders to bond players, spectators, and the band into one."

Looking over her left shoulder to the collection of eager girls behind her, she asked, "Are you all ready?"

Receiving earnest nods of affirmation, she turned to us again. "Everyone will give the same *Victory* cheer individually, and then each group of class candidates will perform the cheer together. We'll collect and total your votes by class and announce the winners. Let's start."

Coach Redding was correct when he said we boys probably had never thought about the girls not having their own sports programs. Nor had we ever consciously revealed our appreciation for all the great things they did on our behalf.

But this event was the one time, each spring, when unknowingly we returned the favor. The annual cheerleading tryout was the only competition girls participated in with the full school involved. Performed in front of students and teachers during an afternoon assembly near the end of every school year, the contest for the following year's squad was determined by students' votes. The winners always consisted of one sophomore, two juniors, and three seniors.

This was the third one I had attended. I loved the atmosphere building up to the final selections. Talk about pressure.

As freshmen voting for our sophomore year, our singular-elected class representative was Sandy Fritz. She was an effervescent petite blonde with a ponytail that responded to every jump and gesture. A superior student, she made an excellent selection to join the same crew as Larry's older sister LaJean for her senior year.

Our two selectees for our junior year were Olinda Odean and Marjane Turner, with Sandy graciously yielding her turn as the focus of attention to begin working hard behind the scenes in the Pep Club. Olinda was one of those unique girls who was everyone's sweetheart. She had it all—looks, intelligence, personality, and poise. Marjane's selection was a surprise to me, as I had not realized the extent of support created by her infectious enthusiasm and extensive Pep Club activities.

Now as juniors, our class could finally select a full quota of three honorees for our senior year.

Several girls began stretching and warming up, wanting the honor of representing her class. My attention was on Trisha Bystrom, Pete's longtime girlfriend.

Pete and Trisha were known as a "couple," having been an item since junior high. Trisha was very attractive, so they made a handsome pairing. They hadn't always actively dated, but even when they weren't, none of us dared ask her out for fear of running afoul of Pete.

But Trisha was her own person, and if anyone could have had a sense of entitlement about a school honor, it would have been she. Her family carried an extra degree of status and stature in town, given her grandfather Morrell Keith Neville had been governor of Nebraska in the early 1900s.

All of us varsity athletes were easily in full support of her, as most of our girlfriends were not in this competition. We were sitting together with Pete in the front left of the auditorium, where we had good visibility of the stage but also had immediate access to our locker room.

I leaned over Larry, who was sitting between Pete and me, and asked them both what they thought Trisha's chances were.

Larry offered, "Great! Her extended family has had season tickets to the high-school football and basketball games forever, and they sit in the same seats year after year. I don't think Trisha has ever missed a game, so she's seen her share of cheerleading. She knows how to do this."

Pete chimed in, "She loves her sports. While growing up, she was quite the tomboy. She's even gone hunting, skeet shooting, and fishing with her grandfather. She's done more things like that than I've done."

Larry asked, "Wasn't she always on the swim team with you, too?"

Pete answered, "Yes. She taught swimming and also did some lifeguarding."

Looking at me, he added, "But her real passion, like Larry said, grew out of years of watching the varsity cheerleaders. She admired their energy and ability to generate enthusiasm with the crowd. She believes the cheerleading squad is an integral part of a team's win-loss record."

Larry smiled. "That's no big deal. I've been watching the cheerleaders closely all that time myself."

Pete and I laughed knowingly, as we had done a little "watching" ourselves.

After our team's demoralizing district basketball loss to Holdrege, I had learned firsthand about Trisha's cheerleader aspiration. In study hall one day not long after that defeat, she had listened to my anguish pour out.

"I say the hell with our Pledge. Coach Redding was right. A piece of paper doesn't win a championship. I thought for certain the Fates would guarantee us a state championship. Now, there's no way it can happen."

She pushed back. "You might not think I know how you feel, but I do. And you might think because I love sports so much I'd be sympathetic to you, but I'm not."

Surprised, I glanced up. Having garnered my attention, she went on, "You can't give up on something you want, just because you fail. Especially if it's important to you and even though it hurts all the more because of that.

"There is nothing I want more than to be a cheerleader. I tried out in junior high, but never made it. The last two years, I tried out to be a junior-varsity or varsity cheerleader and didn't make either one.

"But I'm not going to stop just because it hurts to fail. I'm going to try out again for our senior year."

"Yeah, but our basketball team had worked so hard for it," I countered.

"You think it's easy being a cheerleader? My friends and I worked out for months doing calisthenics and stretching exercises. We practiced endlessly doing all of the cheers and squad routines. This year I've even been working out on a trampoline to improve my jumps. Don't think working hard only applies to you boys."

That was when I first became aware how much of a sport cheerleading was. Trisha had also given me insight into the girls' parallel lives filled with their own ups and downs.

Through that lens, I now watched the girls moving offstage in anticipation of their opportunity to win our votes. I could tell Trisha was nervous.

She looked back toward us. She smiled wryly when Pete gave her a thumbs-up. She knew this was her last chance. Trisha had plenty of recognition in other ways, such as being chosen yearbook editor for our senior year, but not the one thing she wanted most. There was no entitlement present in her wide and bright eyes—only determination.

Receiving the go-ahead from Miss Shields, each girl in turn tackled the designated cheer with gusto. Each received full admiration from the packed auditorium as we noisily supported their courage and desire.

V-I-C-T-O-R-Y
Victory, victory—that's our cry!
Are we in it?
Well, we guess!
North Platte Senior High,
Yes! Yes! Yes!

Spread throughout the auditorium were pockets of exceptionally loud backing for each girl. Each set of friends yelled out encouragement.

The freshmen and sophomore girls did a great job. Any one of them would work out fine as far as I was concerned. This was way more competitive than I had ever remembered or realized.

Trisha was called forward to kick off our junior class's senior-year candidates. She was spectacular, in my opinion. I would have been impressed even if I hadn't been predisposed to liking her performance.

Over our group's concentrated yells and cheers of approval, I heard a bunch of girls' voices behind us, right in the center of the auditorium. I turned to look. It was the Troop. Listening to them, I thought back to their inauguration.

Numbering around twenty strong, the Troop had started in junior high as a small collection of girls in our class who had developed strong friendships. I remember as a freshman, Trisha gave each member a promotional pin—"RAMCO Piston Rings"—from her dad's auto parts business to formalize their association. As a result, the girls all joked Trisha was their "ringleader."

Their group's name came later. One of the girl's spurned boyfriend, after having yet another request for a date being declined because the group offered a prior—or better—commitment, complained that all they did was "troop around together."

The descriptive tag caught on throughout school. Thereafter, a girl's unofficial connection to the Troop became as well known as if she were still wearing a badge proclaiming the fact.

The Troop had rallied itself in full support for its members taking part in the tryouts. Across the classes, there were three, by my count, including Trisha. Great. She needed all the support she could get.

Each of our classmate hopefuls went through her routine, and then they all joined to run through it together one final time. My heart went out to any of them who didn't make it.

"Terrific job!"

"Pete, Trisha did great! She's a lock to get picked."

"Trisha's as good or better than anyone else."

Pete listened to all predictions of success for Trisha, but he barely smiled. He had as much wary intensity in his eyes as if he were getting psyched for a game.

All of a sudden, Coach Best walked out on our side of the stage and looked down at us. On behalf of Coach Redding, he instructed us football and track athletes to leave immediately for weightlifting. As we stood in unison as an automatic response, Pete jumped out in front of us, his palms raised. "You guys, sit down. We need to wait until after the voting."

Pete was not about to leave his longtime friend at this critical moment. He knew how important this was to her.

We all sat down. We cast our votes along with the rest of our classmates and awaited the results, knowing our coaches would be stewing at our noncompliance.

I could see the prospective cheerleaders peek out intermittently through the folds of the curtains at the rear of the stage. Everyone was impatient for the results.

Finally Miss Shields came back up on stage to announce the winners. "Please give me your attention. Thank you for your patience. As I call the names, I'd like the honorees to join me.

"First, from the freshman class for your sophomore year—Vicki Gaibler. Congratulations."

The freshmen all rose up and applauded loudly for Vicki as she ran jubilantly to stand by Miss Shields.

"For the upcoming junior-year selections, I am pleased to announce Marky Charron and Jane Watson!"

Grinning from ear to ear, they rushed to center stage.

Our class stood in anticipation even before the noise died down from the sophomores. A low hum of excited chatter continued.

Miss Shields smiled. "And now for the senior-year choices." Already we juniors were cheering.

"I'm pleased to announce the return this year of Olinda Odean and Marjane Turner!" I could barely hear her add, "This will give our squad a wonderful boost of experience and leadership."

Shouts of "Olinda!" and "Marjane!" echoed throughout the big hall.

Raising her hands to lower the assembly's volume so she could be heard, she continued, "Now it is my extreme pleasure to announce the final member of next year's cheerleading squad. Achieving a position for the first time, please welcome Patricia Bystrom!"

Everyone in our group slapped hands with Pete in congratulations. She had done it. I couldn't imagine how she must have felt to hear her name called after all the years of trying without success.

What I could imagine was that we'd better get our rears in gear. Coach Best had looked none too pleased when we didn't respond to his instructions to leave the auditorium. There would be hell to pay with him and Coach Redding. It would be worth it, though. Besides, wasn't it Coach Redding who said we owed something to the girls?

As Larry and I were striding toward the locker room, we became aware of the increasing crowd noise. We turned and caught sight of Trisha rushing out to accept her new role. We watched as, collapsing into sobs, she was propped up by her new teammates—the Bulldog cheerleading contingent for 1962–1963.

1962–1963 varsity cheerleading squad, *from top to bottom and left to right:*
Marky Charron and Vicki Gaibler; Trisha Bystrom and Marjane Turner;
Jane Watson and Olinda Odean

12

The Man
with the Whistle

Two-a-days, 1962

"**H**ey, Mike," I shouted across the locker room as he walked in. I had arrived early to get suited up to start our second year of two-a-days under Coach Redding. "What happened to you over the summer? You look like you put on fifty pounds of muscle."

He puffed up his chest. "Nah. It was only thirty."

"How did you do it? Last year you were a shrimp at one-thirty. Now you look as big as anyone."

"Weightlifting. Rich Graham and I worked hard all summer, along with some others. Wait until you see him. He's bigger than I am.

"And what about you?" he continued. "You look different, too."

I wrapped my arms around my chest. "I gained twenty pounds— right here. It was my first year working in the haystack on the ranch. Building haystacks was tough work, but now I'm glad I did it."

Mike was right. As the rest of the guys coasted in, each one seemed to be sporting a new body, thanks to a year's growth and working out all summer.

I had already seen Larry the night before, and his regular summer lawn-service business had added ten to fifteen pounds to his already strong frame. The same was true for Pete, as I observed when he

Left: Bob Thomas; *Right:* Rich Graham

walked in. I shuddered, thinking about what full-contact work against him would feel like this year.

Then Rich strolled in, acting as if nothing was unusual. Those of us who hadn't seen him over the summer shouted in unison.

"Rich! Wow!"

"Graham! What happened to you?"

"You have no neck! You're all muscle!"

It was true. He and Mike had transformed themselves. Our two guards were not much taller, but they each now looked like Superman. Opponents might still outweigh them, but no one was going to intimidate them or knock them around.

It was exciting to see everyone again. The changes in physiques created an enthusiasm that sharply contrasted with the apprehension of the year before. Everyone was eager to get to the practice field to show Coach Redding his new and improved team.

After everyone had suited up, we sprinted out together to present ourselves.

Coach had an unsmiling, gruff expression and was standing holding a football with both hands. Positioned on the practice field nearest the game-day field, he was wearing his usual coach's uniform of a white North Platte Athletic Department T-shirt and tan pants with a narrow leather belt. The cuffs were rolled up an extra turn, showing a great deal of white athletic socks before they disappeared into a brand-new set of football cleats. They gleamed in the early morning light.

Coach Redding was again wearing his glass eye along with glasses

Coach George "Crump" Redding

and looked every bit as intimidating as when we first saw him with his black eye patch. Beneath his T-shirt, his muscular chest and arms bulged to remind us of his physicality. The fierce set of his jaw made known he meant business.

Coach Redding blew his whistle to gather us around and to welcome the eighty-plus candidates for the varsity and junior-varsity football teams for the 1962 season.

"Good morning, boys! Yes, we had a good season last year. We surprised a lot of people. But *I* wasn't surprised. I knew what we could do, and now we'll do it even better. This year, there will be no excuses. For those of you juniors and seniors who are returning, you know much more about football than a year ago.

"You know what I expected of you last year, but I promise I will now demand much more. I will work you even harder than last year because I expect us to be at our strongest in the fourth quarter, when our opponents are at their weakest. Those of you on our second string will be better than their second string because our success depends on you. If you commit to being the best you can be, our first stringers will be fighting for their lives to keep their positions.

"You all will have to be better because we won't surprise anyone this time around. We pissed some people off last year who were used to beating up on North Platte teams, and they'll be gunning for you. If I were you, I'd be pretty damned scared, 'cause if I don't get you, then they might."

Last season, Coach Redding buffaloed us because we didn't know what to expect. But now we veterans started to relax. I could see it in my cohorts' body language as they shook their arms to loosen up. We were ready for him this time. When he told us we'd better be afraid of either our opponents or of him, we nudged each other in the back where he couldn't see us.

Bring 'em on, I thought about our opponents.

"Give us your best shot," I heard someone behind me challenge Coach Redding in a whisper.

This year we were a step ahead of him.

After blowing his whistle again, he yelled, "Let's get going! I want to see who kept in shape this summer and who didn't!"

I was confident about showing him. In addition to working harder at my day job on the ranch, I had brought my running shoes to get in some earnest training. I knew what was in store for me. I even ran once a week in my football cleats to get them broken in to prevent blisters later on. It had been reckless of me a year earlier to underestimate how difficult football training would be. I wasn't going to make that mistake again.

In addition to my nightly sprint work, I had added in a mile jog out to the county road. As I ran carefully in the deep ruts, I was thankful I wasn't running in my slippery cowboy boots.

I had conducted my evening workouts intensely in part so I could forget the lingering pain from the Holdrege game, even if only for an hour. Would that ache ever go away?

We got to the calisthenics area before the coaches did, and our co-captains, Larry and Pete, had us in motion without a word. Along with the two of them, we seniors were taking our leadership roles seriously, wanting to set a good example for the younger players.

We combined to form a well-oiled machine, pounding out jumping jacks with precision and running in place with synchronistic, explosive energy.

Intermittent yelps burst from our group as adrenaline built. We were pushing one another to a new level minute by minute. It was exciting. We were eager and well prepared for Coach Redding's two-a-days and his ninety minutes of strictly disciplined fundamentals and skills training.

Or so we thought.

We discovered the man with the whistle always holds ultimate power. It wasn't long before we were bent over, sucking air, grabbing hamstrings and charley horses, and cursing Coach Redding under our labored breath.

And Coach Redding threw us a curve ball from the beginning. In the previous year's two-a-days, we were at least a week into them before we had any full-contact scrimmages. This year we had a full-blown, full-contact scrimmage in our very first practice.

Bob "Punky" Roberts

Although Coach Redding had effectively reasserted his supremacy, our first few practices revealed that a lot within our team was different this year beyond weight gains.

The year before, we had a potential defensive weakness in the middle of our line we never shored up. This year, although we were a senior-dominated team, we had a junior interior lineman who was kicking butt. Bob "Punky" Roberts had served notice he owned that territory.

I remembered him from junior high. He had thoroughly earned his nickname, for he truly was a punk. He smoked and drank and raised hell.

Last year, I was faintly aware Punky had played on the JV team but never thought much about him. This year every one of us was thinking about him.

Punky always had a smile of sorts on his face, and his dark hair was unruly. His countenance seemed to be that of an older person. Even though he wasn't all that tall, whenever I saw him I had the impression of a much bigger man crammed into his body and head. He was definitely someone you wouldn't want to meet in a dark alley.

One night in the weight room, I mentioned Punky and his exceptional play to Larry. "Wow. Punky is something else this year. He is really going to help us. I wonder what made that happen. It's as if he appeared from out of nowhere."

Larry looked around to make sure no one was listening. "Punky has a heckuva story. He comes from a broken family on the north side, and somewhere along the way he and I became friendly. He told me his mom had been prostituting to try and make ends meet. His anger and embarrassment about his family spilled over into all of the things he did that caused us to call him Punky.

"Not surprisingly, he developed severe drinking, grade, and girl-friend problems. More than once I've talked him out of running away or worse."

I'd had no idea.

"You know the Wilson family?" Larry asked. "They took him in, so at least he had a roof over his head and three good meals a day. But he was still struggling emotionally until Coach Redding came to town.

"Punky told me that last year Coach approached him in the hall, saying he wanted to meet the kid who kept beating up his football players in fights. One thing led to another, and Redding took Punky under his wing. Among other things he put him on the JV squad to become part of a team.

"Punky stopped being at the wrong place at the wrong time and started feeling good about himself. It's unbelievable what Coach has done with him."

Finally Punky was making everyone sit up to take notice of him in a positive way. This reminded me of the change Coach Redding caused in Pete's outlook and performance, though Punky's story was even more dramatic because his whole life had shifted.

As the practices continued, I noticed the crowds growing. Last year's football success was infectious, and there was the entertainment value of guessing whose throat Coach Redding was going to jump down next.

As Coach Redding was an equal-opportunity judge of performance, even top players had their moment as the focus of his special attention.

One memorable event occurred when, after becoming upset with Pete's effort in a tackling drill, he lunged at Pete and literally tore his helmet off his head and then verbally ripped into him. When finished, Coach Redding made Pete do several tackling drills against different players until he was satisfied.

Pete, who was a bone-crusher the year before at just under 170 pounds, had become 185 pounds of muscle and resolve. Those of us who were the recipients of Pete's punishment that day hated Coach Redding for taking Pete up another level in effort. After getting the wind knocked out of me a second time, the only good thing I could think about Pete's reprimand was it increased my appreciation for being on his side during games.

But the biggest change for the team involved Larry. He and Pete had been our big 1–2 punch last year, and we all assumed our team's offense this year would center around that same halfback-fullback combo.

With quarterback Bill Stephenson's graduation, Coach Redding had something different in mind. He saw the same thing in Larry we all did: a gifted, all-around athlete; a coach on the field; and someone imperturbable who would always figure out a way to win. We players just accepted that, but Coach Redding knew what to do with it—he changed Larry's position to quarterback. His theory was simple. Get the ball into the hands of the best athlete as often as possible.

Larry was not initially comfortable with the move, as the halfback position had always worked so productively for him. He committed to Coach Redding he would give it his best shot, however, and worked hard at mastering the position.

To take advantage of having a quarterback with Larry's running skills, Coach Redding installed a number of new sweeps and misdirection handoffs. With those plays, we still had Larry and Pete as our 1–2 punch but were now able to get much more variety out of our backfield formation. Coach promised our new diversity would wreak havoc on the opposing teams' defenses.

One of the more subtle changes in the second year under Coach Redding was we were beginning to see more of his dry sense of humor.

He still jumped into the middle of a drill or scrimmage to demonstrate proper technique but wasn't as often able to manhandle us as before. Sometimes when he got knocked down, he'd shake his head and ask someone in mock seriousness, pointing to his glass eye, "Is my eye still in?"

And once when Jim Huffman stepped out of one of the early scrimmages, limping off the field, Coach Redding yelled at him, "Huffman, where are you going?"

Jim meekly answered, "Coach, I hurt my leg."

That just opened the door for Coach Redding's comeback, "Your leg is three feet from your heart! You'll live! Get back in there!"

●　●　●

The days passed quickly, and before we knew it, the first game of our senior year against the Sidney Maroon was upon us. For the season-opening starting lineup, Coach Redding selected Larry, Pete, Allan, and Rodger Tuenge in the backfield, along with Marv and me as ends, Bob Oswald and Jerry James as tackles, pals Mike and Rich as guards, and Jack Edwards at center.

The common denominator among us starters was we were good blockers. If you couldn't block, you wouldn't get much game time.

The newest members of our squad were the Tuenge twins. Rodger started at left halfback, and Rodney was close behind, backing up Rodger and Allan.

Two good-looking farm boys, they had transferred to our high school from nearby Hershey, spending the school weekdays at their grandmother's home in North Platte. I could barely tell the twins apart in school clothes. Put shoulder pads and helmets on them, and I was clueless.

As sophomores on the JV squad, they had initially been slotted at guard positions. As juniors, with the arrival of Coach Redding, they were put back to their familiar running-back positions, which they had learned playing eight-man football at Hershey. The change fit them like a glove, and they were thoroughly reenergized for our senior year season.

Rodney and Rodger Tuenge

They were fearless blockers, so they fit perfectly in Coach Redding's offensive scheme along with Pete at fullback and Allan at right
half. Their toughness on the football field belied the fact they were the
nicest pair of kids you could find.

Another easygoing player was Bob "Ozzie" Oswald. Ozzie had been
alternating with a couple of others at left tackle, and his final selection
surprised me somewhat, as he did not have a mean bone in his body.
Even so, I appreciated having his 210-pound frame next to me.

Jerry James, at the other tackle position, was one tough kid. He
was quiet but always in the right place with plenty of fight in him.

Having a guy like Jerry at right tackle was good because Marv's
playing status at right end was uncertain. Marv caught a gash in his
shin from someone's cleats a few days before and couldn't shake an
infection that set in. I had become used to seeing him tough it out for
a long time with his right upper arm taped tight to his body due to a
year-old shoulder injury. But his leg infection was getting the better of
him. It hurt to watch him hobbling around.

Left: Bob "Ozzie" Oswald; *Right:* Jerry James

Whenever I thought about it, last year's Holdrege-basketball game still hurt. But I was starting to feel something totally unexpected about our football squad that was helping me cope. It was the power of a real team, and something I'd felt previously only in baseball and basketball. This year, when we carried out our scrimmages, whether we starters were playing offense or defense, hints appeared of the same magic we had experienced in the other two sports.

Our offensive plays were sharp and crisp, and everyone was where they should be throughout the whole play. No one stopped until the whistle blew.

On defense, we were scary good. I would have hated to have to play against us. We had no weaknesses. Everyone protected his territory to the death, yet rushed to wherever the ball carrier was headed to gang-tackle him. If we didn't have half a dozen players in the heap as the play ended, we felt like someone was slacking off and made sure everyone's effort was dialed up. Coach Redding often criticized us for a missed opportunity on offense but had few disapproving words for us on defense.

I was liking the overall feeling within the squad.

On the night before the Sidney game as our co-captains gathered us together, Larry captured my sentiments. He said, "We might just have something here."

Larry's statement reminded me of something Coach Redding had written in my yearbook at the end of our junior year.

"It's been interesting in '61–'62. Let's go all the way in '62–'63." He had signed it "Crump."

From author's 1962 school annual: Coach Redding's personal note

13

So Far, So Good

I'd forgotten what it was like to play under the lights. It was as if all my senses had been plugged into the same electrical current. I could hear and sense the crowd, which was almost as large as last year's afternoon championship game, but the illumination kept my visual attention focused on the field.

We were going through our pregame warm-ups for our first game of the year, and I couldn't help but observe the Sidney Maroon players doing the same.

The sensation reminded me of when I was a little boy attending an evening rodeo performance. Sitting in the dark with the rodeo grounds brightly lit, I was filled with excitement. I knew something exhilarating and unexpected would soon happen with short bursts of action from cowboy and beast.

My heightened consciousness also had a fresh, unfamiliar side. In junior-high football, my pregame awareness was fear based, whereas now I was the hunter rather than the hunted.

I felt good. I had a job to do, a role to play. My teammates were counting on me to do my part. Besides, Coach Redding would kill me worse than any opponent if I fell short of what he expected and needed from me.

My buddies had prepared well for their final season and made unbelievable improvements in their capabilities. Our linemen were strengths for us rather than weaknesses. One short year ago I did not believe we could ever field a team like this. Those pipsqueak boys I used to know always had the will, determination, and love for sports. Now each possessed the body to back it up. I wouldn't let them down.

The game was about to begin.

As we gathered around Coach Redding, I looked at my teammates. I didn't see football players. I saw friends whose strengths and weaknesses had been revealed in ways we never expected. As a result we had to learn to accept and compensate for each other.

Something else about them was both different and familiar. They were confident of themselves, of each other, and of our coach. It was that same simplistic, passionate assumption of what's going to happen next that we possessed in baseball and basketball, but never before in football.

Sidney had achieved the Class B state championship the previous year with an undefeated record. Even though they lost a few key players to graduation, we still expected a tough game.

Our offense started slowly, but we eventually earned a 28–0 shutout on the strength of our defense. On offense, Larry, Pete, and Allan each scored touchdowns on runs, and I scored one on a short pass from Larry.

As we had the season before, we ran for our extra points instead of kicking them. We were successful on all four conversions, with Larry scoring three points-after-touchdowns and Pete scoring one.

I felt we had a well-balanced effort for it being our first game of the season.

The following Monday night was our first game-film review. It was always an interesting way to spend an evening. Homework would have to wait until Redding had his say.

"All right, boys. I've looked at the film, and we've got a lot of work to do, so let's get to it.

"First, Pete—good job running the ball, but you'll see plenty of instances where you could have gotten more yardage by just plowing ahead. And Wachholtz, for chrissakes, call your own number out there more often. That's what you're there for. If all you do is hand off to the backs, the defenses will settle in and lock us up."

I was eager to watch myself on film and became excited when Coach started the projector. Then he launched into his analysis.

"Graham! What kind of titty block was that? You barely touched him!

"Kirkman, that play is designed for you to pull out and block someone, not stumble on Edwards's feet and fall down! And Jack, if you're going to fall down, too, at least fall forward so you stay out of the way.

"Tatman! How on earth did I think you had a good game running the ball? James and Binegar opened up a perfectly good hole for you if only you had decided to hustle. Get off your ass! They can't hold their blocks forever!

"Thomas, next time you're going to run downfield to pretend to make a block and then just roll around on the field, run far enough away so you're out of camera range. I don't want to have to look at that shit. You make me want to puke!"

And so it went. One long slog through every play, with each slipped block and weak arm tackle and lazy effort called out. It took forever and felt like we hadn't done anything right.

I wondered why I had been looking forward to watching the film. I had to remind myself we won the game. How could I have forgotten what a perfectionist pain in the ass he was?

Our second game of the season was with our first West Division foe at Kearney, and we ran away with it, 40–12. Everyone made it into the game, which was unusual since Coach Redding generally stuck with his starters. Participating was beneficial for the second-team's attitude and a nice reward for working hard without publicity.

The Kearney game-film review went much better.

Our assumption going into the game was Kearney would struggle this year, so we knew we shouldn't get too excited over the big score differential. But our offense had appeared to be nicely balanced. And our first two games had confirmed the strength of our defense. Overall, my impression was we were developing on schedule.

Two games into the season, it was time for the *Omaha World-Herald*'s first state rankings to be published. Looking at McBride's Sunday newspaper column, I was shocked to find our team in a lofty number-four position. I hadn't figured on a top-five ranking! I was just hoping to see our team in the top ten.

I didn't know what to make of it, other than we were no longer going to surprise our opponents. I wondered what Coach Redding was going to say at practice on Monday.

I soon had my answer.

"Gregg McBride doesn't know what he's talking about! If we're the number-four team in the state, I'll eat my hat!"

Without a game scheduled for that week, the coaches took stock of how we individually stood in our intrasquad rankings in the Bulldog Club. The club was an individual recognition program brought by Coach Redding and was based on a point system heavily weighted toward defense. The first twenty-five points earned a player a Bulldog decal to put on his helmet, and each twenty-five points thereafter earned a star to apply next to the Bulldog.

The season before, only four players had qualified for a Bulldog decal, with Pete being the only honoree from our class. The point totals carried over from last season, so Pete had thirty-seven points and was working on his first star.

As a result of the Kearney game, Allan earned his membership. Coach Redding convened a team ceremony for Allan after practice and recapped the point criteria.

"Allan became a part of our Bulldog Club with twenty-eight points, so I will remind you how you can join him.

"You earn half a point for every assisted tackle, and a full point each for unassisted tackles, fumble recoveries, and interceptions. And if you really want to jump ahead fast, you can earn two points each for blocking opponents' punts or point-after kicks, for making a downfield block that springs a runner for a touchdown, or for making a *demolition derby*. As a reminder, a *demolition derby* is when you make a clean block or tackle that knocks the opposing player out of the game for at least one play.

"Coach Johnson, would you do the honors and present Allan with his decal?"

As Assistant Coach Johnson put the decal on Allan's helmet, Allan looked as if he would explode with pride.

Larry was on the cusp of club membership with twenty-four points, and I was getting close with twenty-one. I wanted that decal plastered on my helmet in front of the whole squad. I wanted some of that.

Even though we were idle in the third week of the season, we benefited in the rankings by upsets across the state, which resulted in our climbing one notch in the rankings to third place. Leapfrogging us to number two, however, was our opponent for the coming week, Hastings.

Hastings was sporting a strong 3–0 start for the year. They were certain to be more than a little eager to pay us back for our beating them the previous year in the conference championship. They still had many of the great athletes we had seen before, including their talented end, Tom Smith, and their headliner, Wayne Weber. Weber was touted as one of the top three all-around athletes in the state, along with Larry and Scottsbluff's Gary Neibauer. Not surprisingly, all three played quarterback.

Hastings entered the game without the services of Chuck Stickles, who played end opposite Smith. Normally providing a huge presence with his 6' 7" height, Stickles was out with an injury, but we had our own problems. Pete had a stomach ailment, Allan had a sprained wrist, and Marv was still smarting from his leg infection. Despite their problems, all three of our guys talked Max into getting the doctor's approval for them to play along with the rest of us.

A full-capacity hometown Hastings crowd of four thousand fans came to help push their team to a 13–7 advantage at the half. Everyone in Hastings was eager to see us go down.

Our locker room's mood at halftime was somber, but Coach Redding surprised us with his calmness. "This is no surprise," he reassured us. "We knew these boys were good and would come out strong. But they've taken their best shot, and we've held up well. The second half belongs to us!"

As defensive end, my responsibility was to make deep penetration into their backfield as quickly as possible after the snap from center. In doing so, I had come close all during the first half to intercepting Weber's wide pitchouts to his halfback on my side.

Early in the second half, I finally got to one while they were on their 35-yard line. I knocked it away and recovered it at their 18-yard line. We moved on in to score.

With the change in momentum, we scored three more times, giving us a solid 32–20 victory over a quality team.

McBride had attended the game, and his subsequent weekend articles were filled with respect for Coach Redding and our team. He was most impressed with Pete on defense and Larry on offense.

By McBride's account, Pete was in on seemingly every tackle. He noted Larry scored two touchdowns and threw for another, while also returning kickoffs and punts for big yardage. McBride included comments from Coach Redding, who called out Marv, Punky, and Allan for additional recognition.

But the big news was McBride moved our team into the top position in his poll. North Platte went crazy.

Before Coach Redding arrived in town, there had been countless years of futility. Now the talk in town and throughout school was that Crump's team was North Platte's best ever.

Coach Redding had lost his underdog status, and he took it out on us. "You guys had better not be reading your own press clippings. You are far from being the top team in the state. McBride just got carried away because he attended the game. Now everyone will be gunning for us the rest of the season, trying to knock us off our lofty perch."

Admittedly, we thought we were pretty good. We were proud of our top billing. But there was no thought of adopting basketball's "State by '63!" goal for football. It never occurred to us, even though eight of the original thirteen signees of the basketball pledge were members of the varsity football team.

Football in North Platte had been so bad for so long, all we wanted to do was win as many games as we could. The ranking was gravy. A state championship was inconceivable.

After the Hastings game, Larry and I joined Pete and Allan as members of the Bulldog Club, with Pete earning his first star. Mike was close, with Marv and Punky not far behind.

It was just a decal, but the pride I felt when Assistant Coach Folsom formally put it on my helmet in front of the team made me think my chest was going to burst. My helmet suddenly seemed larger and more like a weapon. I could hardly wait to plant my decal in some runner's gut when he tried to run around my end.

As Larry received his, he looked just like I felt, yet with genuine humility. I was not humble. I was filled with self-importance.

As I watched Larry, I automatically studied him. His youthful Germanic features had always displayed a quiet confidence, but even more so now. Under the demands of Coach Redding to lead the team from a new position, he had grown more in the last month than any time I could remember.

He had made the quarterback position his. I could not imagine anyone else being quarterback. He led with few words, but his body language told every one of us that he was in charge. He walked purposefully, solidly connected to the ground. He talked efficiently and crisply, like an adult. When looking at you, he held your gaze intently.

Using our highest compliment, I decided he definitely was an *animal*.

"Hey, Bob, way to go. It took us long enough to get this damned Bulldog, didn't it?"

● ● ●

Our next contest was against Alliance. It turned out to be a quiet game most notable for the heavy rainfall throughout. That game gave Coach Redding another opportunity to use a large number of players as we were in command the whole way and won 33–0.

Before we knew it, a week had passed, and we had another undefeated team waiting for us. The McCook Bison, at 4–0, had the same perfect record as ours. The game would be on their home turf, and they would be further inspired by it being their Homecoming Day.

Example of Burma-Shave's roadside signs, circa 1960s

As we traveled south to McCook, we were greeted by a parade of signs along the highway set up in Burma-Shave fashion. We were familiar with the national advertising program that used witty promotional slogans on small signs placed atop roadside fence posts to tout Burma-Shave's shaving cream.

Using Burma-Shave's style of piecemeal jingles, McCook had created its own phrases to predict North Platte's destruction. We read each set of signs with interest and enjoyment.

Many of the slogans were amusing and clever. Due to our chuckling at them, the effort probably served its purpose and distracted us.

A record crowd of 4,100 attended after enjoying a parade of floats. With the floats staged alongside the field, I noticed the winner was one titled "Gregg McBride's Typewriter."

It was a farm implement—a manure spreader—barely spruced up with tissue paper and streamers to look like a float. The ironic thing about the intended slight was that McBride, who had again traveled from Omaha to watch our game, had forecast in his column the McCook Bison would come out victorious.

Their strong team demonstrated the validity of their record and played us tough early in the game. They drove the ball to a first and goal at our one-yard line on their first possession. Successive defensive gems by Mike, Pete, and Punky sent them reeling back and allowed our team to collect ourselves as we took over on downs. We eventually scored a touchdown on that drive.

Just before the half, Larry found Pete open for a fifty-yard touchdown pass that helped widen the halftime margin to 13–0.

Coach Redding was so upset with our overall play in the first half, however, he didn't take us into the locker room. He had us sit in the south end zone while he raked us over the coals.

Our focus sharpened, we hit fast and often in the second half and played our game the way we were taught. Playing our best football of the season, we ended up dominating 39–7 with Pete being the star of the game offensively as well as defensively.

Coach Redding was also proving himself to us in a new way. We had known him to be a great practice coach in teaching fundamentals and getting us prepared to play an opponent. But we were beginning to also appreciate his game-coaching skills. With great skill he could pick apart what we were doing or not doing, and he could do the same with our opponents.

It was impossible to overemphasize the advantage it gave us to believe Coach Redding would always be there during a game with the right answer. We were able to play fearlessly through any difficulties.

Still carrying our number-one ranking after the McCook game, it was time for our own Color Day/Homecoming. We were to host our nemesis, Grand Island, the one team that had physically punished us in the prior season.

By the end of the game, Coach Redding was finally happy with the way Punky and Pete played.

Their big fullback, Stan Farrar, had graduated, but they had a fine array of athletes and the same strong offensive line. We knew their team would give us fits if we weren't sharp, but that was going to be more problematic than usual due to our having multiple lineup changes for the game.

Coach Redding got mad at Rodger during practice for some shortcoming not obvious to the rest of us, so he was demoted. His twin brother Rodney was assigned to take his place. Allan was injured, so junior Herb Weichman would start for him. Ozzie had been shifted to play center, so Terry Hunt, a strong junior at 180 pounds, looked like he would be my blocking mate at left tackle for the rest of the season.

Mike would also be missing from action. He hurt his leg during the McCook game and showed up at school Monday on crutches. He ran into Coach Redding coming out of the boiler room, where the male teachers congregated to smoke and tell stories. To hear Mike tell it, Coach was none too happy to see him on crutches and gave him an earful. Max had apparently forgot to tell Coach he had prescribed the crutches. In any event, Punky, along with his defensive responsibilities, would start at offensive guard for Mike.

We all knew Grand Island would be a tough team to go up against with so many lineup changes.

It was a cold, windy, and rainy night, which must have made for a miserable coronation of our Color Day queen, Olinda Odean, and her two attendants, Vicki Gaibler and Rae Ellen Geis. We missed most of their halftime ceremonies, being involved in a solemn halftime assessment at the time. We had the lead at 7–0, but Grand Island was far too strong a team for us to feel comfortable.

The playing conditions were so bad and uncomfortable, it was difficult to keep the importance of winning the game at the top of our consciousness. The temptation was constantly present to surrender to our discomfort and let the game's outcome be damned. In the end, however, we were able to hurry back to our warm homes to thaw out as victors. We had prevailed, 14–0, thanks to another strong defensive showing and a balanced offense.

Left: Coach Redding sends Rodney back into action with instructions.
Right: Terry Hunt

Allan got in for a few plays and scored one touchdown on a twenty-two-yard pass, and Pete had scored the second touchdown on a short burst up the middle. Coach Redding eventually let Rodger back in the game, but it had been Rodney's night, and he definitely held up his end of the bargain.

We stood at 6–0 for the season and were solidly positioned as the number-one ranked team in the state. Hastings had rebounded from its only loss to us and was ranked right behind us. If we both held our positions through the next two games, we would play again not only for the Big Ten championship but for the state championship as well. It was pretty heady stuff and a real challenge not to get caught up in the "what-ifs."

Coach Redding would not let us rest on our laurels and get ahead of ourselves, though. We had a job to do first, and that was to win the West Division title by defeating Scottsbluff. To accomplish that, we had to play the game at Scottsbluff, where they would be doubly tough. This was a rivalry where records and past performances meant nothing. Mike was still out with his injury, so Roberts would have to do double duty again.

Coach Redding had us ready, and we led at halftime, 19–7.

One of the more humorous plays of the season occurred just before the end of the first half. As Gary Neibauer prepared to punt with the clock running down, his coach yelled out to him, "Don't kick it to Wachholtz! Don't let him have a chance to return the ball!"

No doubt Gary intended to comply, but his natural instincts took over, and he blasted his best punt of the game right into Larry's arms on our 48-yard line. Fifty-two yards later, Larry tossed the ball to the official in the end zone to give us a near two-touchdown halftime advantage, with the Scottsbluff coach ready to commit hara-kiri.

The weather turned cold and stormy just before halftime, so when Coach Redding entered the locker room, he took his socks off and put them on a stove in the back of the room so they could dry out. He then became absorbed in running through all of the things he felt we had done wrong in the first half and would need to do better in the second half.

As he was deep into his halftime critique, Pete, sitting by the stove, interrupted. "Coach . . . ? Coach!"

Coach Redding, without looking in his direction, growled, "Shut up, Pete. I'll get to you in a minute!"

Twice more Pete called out, only to be shut down by Coach each time. Finally the socks, which had been smoldering, burst into flames.

With our halftime huddle cut short by the smoke and the smell, we rushed back to the field.

We scored once more and barely held on as they closed strong, led by Neibauer's heroics. We'd made just enough significant plays to win, including Rodger's forty-yard run for a touchdown, Larry's eighteen-yard run and punt return for touchdowns, and a twenty-three-yard pass I hauled in from Larry for a touchdown. That pass was our final score and gave us the closing winning margin of 26–21.

Undefeated at 7–0, the West Division championship was ours. We had earned a repeat ticket to the Big Ten championship game.

Only one non-conference school, Gering, stood between us and a perfect regular-season record that would give us a chance to also be playing for the state championship in our Big Ten championship game. For the first time we started thinking in earnest about the bizarre possibility of our being football state champs.

So far, so good.

14

You Don't Always Get What You Deserve

Seven games into the season, I was gratified our team was making good on our potential. In a self-satisfied mood, I read the newspaper summaries of our season. I figured it wouldn't hurt to reflect on our collective accomplishments to date.

I learned we had rushed for almost 1,800 net yards while holding our opponents to well under 900 yards. While passing far less than our opponents, we had still gained over 500 yards to their measly 300 yards. We had not been scored on at home all year. Pete had not suffered one instance of losing yardage all year long. Five of our backs had averaged over five yards per carry. The list went on and on.

As one result, many sportswriters and pundits regularly tabbed Larry and Pete as the strongest 1–2 backfield combination in conference history and possibly in state history as well.

We might just be state-championship quality after all, I decided. What if we were to win the football title and then go on to fulfill our long-held basketball pledge? I was delirious with the possibility of two state championships.

Having already played all of the preseason projected competitive and worrisome teams on our schedule, all that remained of our regular season was an easy waltz scheduled with Gering. After that presumed victory, we would be undefeated for the year. We would earn a shot at the state championship in our Big Ten title game the following week, a repeat engagement with number-two ranked Hastings on their home field.

Throughout the week leading up to the game with Gering, Coach Redding kept hounding us not to look ahead to Hastings. He claimed Gering had good athletes and pointed out they had only one loss all year.

But how many times did he expect us to fall for that old coach's trick? For Scottsbluff, maybe, but for Gering? Gering had three starters sidelined due to injuries. With Mike healed up, we were back to full strength.

The game would be on our home turf. That was our land.

All the state's sportswriters agreed we vastly outmatched Gering. Sure, we had to play the game, but there wasn't any doubt who the winner would be.

Finally the night arrived for the game. I wanted to get it behind us so we could get on with preparing for our title game.

With the evening being Father's Night, our dads were seated along the south half of our sideline. Each was proud to be a more intimate part than usual of the team's season-long success and pending victory. Their folding chairs were lined up close enough to the field for us to touch their outstretched hands as we ran through our pregame drills.

Railroad men, farmers, salesmen, and businessmen . . . Even Jim Kirkman came down from the press box to sit with the other dads that special night. For many of our fathers, it was the first time they had been this near the team, and I could see their bashfulness mixed with pride.

It was neat to see the older generation of my buddies all in one place. I knew we would put on a helluva show for them.

As we gathered around Coach Redding for final pregame instructions, we were only distantly engaged for the task ahead of hosting Gering on that cold November evening.

Gering neglected to read our version of the script, however, and came ready to play the best game of their season. Before we realized what was happening, Gering engineered their first possession from my opening kickoff into a drive we finally stopped on our four-yard line with a timely fourth-down stand.

We took possession, but Gering's 190-pound tackle, Pete Johnson, immediately broke through our offensive line on our first play to throw Pete Tatman for a loss and a safety. That had to have been a mistake. Those things didn't happen to us.

Gering led 2–0.

I kicked off again following the safety, and Gering promptly marched straight down the field. This time they rammed the ball into the end zone for a touchdown and an 8–0 lead!

For chrissakes! Their potent drive was no mistake. Play by play they had overpowered us. At least we foiled their PAT attempt.

I wasn't the only one shaken by the unlikely turn of events. After returning Gering's kickoff, Larry, for the first time all season and for as long as I could remember, seemed flustered as we gathered in the offensive huddle. I thought maybe he got tackled extra hard.

Mike finally broke the awkward silence by quietly suggesting, "Let's run 31 off me."

After a few plays, we recaptured a little momentum offensively. Yet, for the rest of the first half, all that was accomplished was both teams traded goal-line stands. The score at halftime reflected our continued deficit of 8–0, and the sad and disturbing truth was it should have been much worse.

The halftime discussion was grim, as it was obvious our dour situation was no fluke. The Gering team was simply outplaying us, and there was no sign of their relenting. I could see everyone was as sick as I was at the idea of our season being flipped upside down.

Coach Redding laid into us. "You thought you could coast against this team. You believed you deserved a victory and assumed it would happen automatically.

"Run the plays the way you've been taught. Cooperate on defense the way you've been taught. They are doing nothing unusual. They're just playing old-fashioned kick-ass football and daring you to stop them.

"You let them get your goat, and they know it. Now you're going to have to work twice as hard to take away their confidence. And, somebody block that Johnson character."

We individually went about the business of absorbing the coach's criticism to regenerate the focus and commitment that should have been there at the start of the game. We were finally paying attention. I hoped it wasn't too late.

With more resolve, we garnered our first score early in the third quarter on a short run by Pete. We then took our first lead of the game early in the fourth quarter, thanks to a forty-yard pass from Larry to me, followed by Pete's PAT.

The score stood at 13–8 in our favor at last. The natural order of things had been restored. Gering would comprehend the inevitable, give up the ghost, and slip peacefully into the night.

But what was the problem with them? They kept coming at us. Didn't they know what a loss would do to us?

After a couple of possession changes, Gering again forced us to punt, and their Rich Iliff slipped through our line and blocked the punt. Two plays later, with 3:03 left to play in the game, Gering scored on a pass play to lead 14–13. I wasn't sure I knew what the "natural order" was anymore.

After Gering's subsequent kickoff, we started on our 34-yard line on the north side of the field, faced with a one-point deficit. We had to score on that possession, or Gering would win. It was that simple.

There were no timeouts left. Despite Coach's attempts to calm us down from the sideline, I had a deepening sense of dread. This felt like a repeat of the Holdrege basketball game. Would losing the big ones be our legacy?

Larry shook off his earlier discomfiture and salvaged a long run off a broken pass play to get into Gering's territory. He completed a 24-yard pass to me to get our team to Gering's 24-yard line with 2:19 to go in the game.

First down.

Larry called for a quarterback sweep around Marv's side, making it to the 10-yard line.

First down.

As the clock kept ticking, he called the same play again in the huddle. We all flinched and glanced up at him in surprise, but there was no time to question him as he quickly broke the huddle. As the play launched, there was furious blocking going on. Larry wound his way to his right through the holes created in the defense, scoring the go-ahead touchdown.

We had done it. *Larry* had done it. We had taken the lead and were actually going to win this thing.

Hold it. Not so fast. Two officials' flags were on the ground. Those blind, biased bastards had called a fifteen-yard clipping penalty on us.

I watched in disbelief as the play was called back and the ball placed on the 25-yard line. All I could think was, Holy shit!

It was still first down, but we were now twenty-five yards away from a victory and a perfect regular season.

The clock read 1:39 remaining. We were staring at defeat and crushing disappointment. This definitely was Holdrege all over again. No way could I take another devastating humiliation like that.

We valiantly ran back to form up the huddle, where Larry at least called a different play, sending Rodger around my side for a thirteen-yard gain. All of us were blocking as we never had before.

Second down.

Larry had run over during the play to get instructions from Coach. We rushed back to the huddle with the clock running, expecting Larry to call a pass play. Instead, he called the same quarterback sweep around right end we had run two out of the last three plays. We all jerked up and looked over at him as if to say, "Are you nuts? We aren't going to fool anyone! We don't have time to keep running the ball!"

Larry simply said, "Get me some damned blocks." The piercing look in his eyes shut down the rebellion and got us back in focus.

The whole season was coming down to a black-or-white situation. Either we scored on the next couple of plays to keep our season's hopes alive, or we didn't and our dreams would die.

Ozzie snapped the ball to Larry, and everyone picked someone to block. From my left-end position, I raced downfield to my left to fake a pass play to hold the defensive secondary in place a few extra seconds. Then I ran back across the field as fast as I could to come up from behind to help with a downfield block.

There was no need for my intended heroics, as everything was handled. Marv and the right side of the line blocked down toward the center. Pete, Allan, and Rodger blocked out toward the sidelines. Just as I came up to help, Larry faked the two remaining defenders out of position, leaving them rolling in the dust.

I had the perfect positioning to escort Larry into the end zone.

There were no flags this time, and we all collected around him and pounded his shoulder pads in gratitude for his supreme athletic accomplishment.

But this time, even though we had scored a touchdown and PAT to lead 20–14, there was no premature rejoicing about this game being over. There had been so many twists and turns, we were all-business concerning the time remaining.

I kicked off, and we covered it expertly, stopping them at their 14-yard line with less than a minute to go. After four incomplete Gering passes, the game clock ran out of time. The game was ours. Improbably, yes, but ours. Deservedly, no, but ours.

Coach Redding, all of us players, all of our dads, and everyone in the stands looked numb. We had come too close to being defeated to celebrate. We were grateful and relieved for overcoming a powerful and inspired effort by the Gering team, coached by Mert Van Newkirk.

This was one time we were fortunate we didn't get the outcome we deserved. We were flat-out lucky to have survived.

All present at the game also realized they had witnessed something rare from Larry. He put the team and the game on his back and carried us where we could not have otherwise traveled. If there had ever been any non-believers about his towering and unique athletic capabilities, his performance in our final offensive series of the game converted them.

Larry's attitude and "do-over" touchdown finally allowed me to identify the element of athleticism Larry had the rest of us did not. He had a place within him where he could go, where he visualized a

Larry's uncle, Hop Gilster, and cheerleader Jane Watson, congratulate Larry.

different outcome than conditions indicated—the outcome in which he wanted to be involved. He then proceeded single-mindedly to write his new future.

We mingled with our dads. Everyone was in shock. I had discovered what the phrase "dodging a bullet" meant.

Grateful smiles began to show on our fathers' faces as they offered praise and congratulations to Larry, but the rest of us boys were solemn and kept our helmets on. We had to face Coach Redding when we got back to the locker room.

Coach was pissed, emotional. He grabbed Ozzie by the face bar on his helmet, pulled him over to a bench, and then ripped the helmet off his head. He motioned everyone to sit down. Jack made the mistake of lowering his head, and Coach bopped him hard with Ozzie's helmet to get his attention. It worked—for all of us.

Coach spat out, "That was disgusting. I'm embarrassed!"

He gathered himself and started over. "People paid good money to attend this game, and all they saw was you farting around all night. They think the way you played is the way you've been taught to play. Bullshit!"

Coach was heating up. "They went through you linemen like a sieve, tackling Tatman in the end zone for a safety! Do you toughen up after that? No! You stand aside like cowards and let them block a punt, for chrissakes!

"Johnson and Iliff and the rest of them manhandled you boys all night like you were on the junior-varsity team. I hate to think what would have happened if their quarterback hadn't gotten hurt before the half and had been able to play the rest of the game.

"You were so proud of yourselves. Never been scored on at home, and all that other horseshit you read all week. First, you gave up that safety, and then you let them score easily on their next possession. Forgot to stop reading about how good you are and patting each other on the back long enough to handle your responsibilities!

"And here I thought I and the other coaches taught you better than this. Maybe you didn't want it bad enough. Did the pressure get to you? Or did you just not give a damn?

"Either way, I don't care. You linemen from tackle to tackle—you're done. You didn't want to work hard enough to play for the championship, so you don't have to. You can take it easy this week as I prepare your backups to take on Hastings. You've forfeited your right to have the honor of being the starting line in a state-championship game.

"Go home and get out of my sight."

Escaping into the showers, we talked quietly and agreed we needed to meet in Larry's basement as soon as we got dressed. Larry's home was southwest from the school, just past the practice field, so those of us without cars got there as quickly as those who drove.

Larry's mom broke out cookies and pies from her freezer, heated them up and brought them downstairs as we quietly gathered around. There was none of our usual horseplay.

Mike started it off. "I'm sorry, guys. Johnson had my number all night. I've never been beaten up like that, play after play. I shouldn't hold down a starting position after a performance like that."

Rich kicked in, "I've never seen anything like it. It seemed like they were a half-count ahead of our snap all night. What the hell did those guys eat before the game? Who the devil were they, anyway?"

"We weren't ready," Pete pointed out. "*I* wasn't ready. We didn't pay any attention to Coach about how tough Gering would play us. He knew, and we would have, too, if we had listened to him like before. We just got cocky and . . ."

As Pete's voice trailed off, we all knew what could have been.

Larry picked it up from there. "OK, let's take this experience and learn from it. I don't know if Coach is going to bench some of us or not, but regardless, we've got to get ready for Hastings next week. Let's go around the room and let everyone say what's on his mind."

The emotion flowed out as comments alternated between looking back to Gering and looking ahead to Hastings. It was a good exercise. My sense of self-importance was knocked down a peg or two as I realized a game's outcome depended on eleven different wars all going on at the same time. The matchups facing each of us on offense and defense were ours alone to win.

I also saw where others experienced the game much differently from the one I thought was occurring. I'd never been inside Marv's head and had never realized although we played the same position at opposite ends of the line, he saw and felt the game totally different than did I.

The one subject we all agreed on was we owed our season's reprieve to Larry.

"Thanks, Larry!"

"Man, you saved our ass out there."

"I thought you were crazy when you called that sweep again!"

"You could have run like that a little sooner so we wouldn't have had to worry like we did!"

Challenged by the good-natured jab, Larry came right back with, "Sure, and if anyone would have occasionally thrown a block out there or made a tackle every once in a while tonight, it wouldn't have come down to that."

Good. Our razzing nature was returning. We were in a better place than when we arrived an hour before. The Gering game and our shortcomings were starting to drift away, and our old competitive and fun-seeking spark was coming back, allowing us to start focusing on Hastings.

Jerry asked no one in particular, "Do you think Coach will really keep us demoted for the game?"

Pete answered. "I don't know. He seems serious, but I can't imagine him not going with you guys in such a big game."

It would be an interesting week coming up at practice.

15

Brass Ring

We were chasing our third Big Ten conference title in a row. As juniors we had helped claim both the football and basketball titles. As seniors, we could grab a second football title in as many years, with the Nebraska state championship also available for the taking.

During the week of preparation for our big game, Coach Redding stuck to his guns and had the former second-team linemen practice with the starting backfield. From what I could see with the replacements, they were as concerned about the situation as were the guys who were demoted. I hoped Coach knew what he was doing.

Coach Redding was calm and focused. He had won a state championship before, so we placed our confidence in him. Lineup issues aside, we did not change our daily practice routine one iota.

I understood his problem with us. All year long we had played as an extension of his personality—volatile, emotional, and aggressive, yet purposeful at the same time.

But in the Gering game, with the whole town watching and so much riding on the outcome, we embarrassed him. By not giving Gering their due as he warned us, we made it clear we thought we knew better and were entitled to a victory.

Had we lost his trust? If so, we had only a handful of days to reestablish it. Maybe at the same time we could get our usual starting line back in action.

Midweek newspaper articles reiterated North Platte had won only two Big Ten football titles since the Big Ten conference had been formed in 1945. Hastings had never won a football title, having lost in the title game three times, including the previous year to us.

For us to win back-to-back conference titles, we would have to beat Hastings twice in the same season on their home field, and we would have to have beaten them three times out of four games over two seasons. They were a strong and motivated team who would not want those statistics to play out. It was going to be a battle.

As the days went by, there was no indication from Coach he would change his mind on the starting lineup. He was either set in concrete or intent upon driving home his point especially hard.

Thursday night, Coach called us together in the locker room as we finished dressing after our showers. I was sure he was gathering us to talk about the starting lineup.

"Boys, stick around. I've asked your co-captains to meet with you so you can talk about the game. We coaches will be out of here shortly. I'll have my time with you tomorrow. Good night."

I was surprised he had gone home with the main issue on our minds still dangling.

After the coaches left, Pete asked the demoted players, "How are you guys doing about not starting?"

The five guys with whom we had waged war on the field now fought to find the right words.

Mike began. "I'm OK. I don't question Coach Redding on his decision. I know I deserved the demotion. As for the guys who are replacing us, they've done a great job in practice and I think they'll do just as good as we would in the game."

His usual running mate at the other guard position, Rich Graham, chimed in. "I won't pretend it's not hard. I'm ashamed. But I agree with Mike. Our replacements will do great. I'll be ready to help out in any way I can." Rich's words sounded better about things than his grim countenance looked.

Jerry said, "Don't worry about us. Our heads are in the game, and we've worked hard at giving the other guys a tough workout this week to get them ready."

Ozzie agreed. "I'm in, no matter what. The game is what's important now."

Terry added, "Yes, Hastings is what it's all about."

Larry let the responses soak in for all of us and then spoke up. "We've got a lot of things to talk about, but the main reason Coach wanted us to meet with you is to give you the starting lineup."

Was that a slight smile starting to appear upon his face?

Drawing out his moment as long as he could, he blurted, "You guys are in! Coach Redding says he's never been more proud about how both groups of linemen reacted to the lineup change. He says we could win with either group, but he's decided to go with experience and asks everyone to accept his decision."

Pete added, "Way to go, guys! Coach talked to the others already, and they're on board. Sorry to make you have to wait so long to hear the news. There's only one thing left to do, and that's to go get Hastings!"

Mike, Rich, Jerry, Terry, and Ozzie humbly accepted the team's congratulations.

"Hooray for you, Mike."

"We knew it would happen, Ozzie."

"Jerry, go take it out on Hastings."

"Rich—way to go!"

"Good for you, Terry," I said as I grabbed him from the side and shook him back and forth. His eyes were lowered and gleaming from emotional appreciation and relief.

I felt sorry for the second-string guys, but at least Coach had spoken to them. The first-stringers would provide our best overall lineup, though, and each would be extra hungry for another chance to prove himself.

● ● ●

Friday, November 9, 1962. Game day. The Nebraska state football championship was at stake.

The *Telegraph-Bulletin* had summarized the pregame matchups analyzed in the major statewide newspapers. The consensus gave a slight nod to our offense on the strength of our backfield combo of Larry and Pete, who had burnished their vaunted reputations without fail throughout the season.

Our defense was also given a slight edge. It was anchored up the middle by Punky on the line, then Pete at linebacker, and finally Larry at safety. Let them try to run or throw elsewhere, though. It wouldn't matter. Our whole defensive crew was incredibly strong at every position.

Hastings had both the home-field and underdog advantages, however, as well as exceptional athletes at each of their skill positions.

All of the competing trade-offs thus rendered the over-all pregame prognostications a toss-up in most analysts' opinions. Our two teams, ranked first and second in the state, would enter the game as close as two teams could be.

We finally knew who would comprise our starting line, and our backfield was the same as it had been all season.

We also knew Hastings's starting lineup by heart. It seemed we had been playing against the same guys in big games forever. Hastings would once more showcase their two offensive stars, quarterback Wayne Weber and end Tom Smith, along with their defensive centerpiece, 195-pound lineman Henry Dilly.

Everyone on both teams was healthy enough to play.

We also had our own supporting army on the way for the battle. School was dismissed at ten o'clock so students could travel to Hastings in time for the two-thirty kickoff.

Because North Platte was a railroad town, a special train was easily commissioned from Union Pacific. Over five hundred people boarded, including our seventy-five-piece marching band. On top of that, a number of buses and a huge caravan of cars made the journey. Numbering over one thousand, our supporters were doing everything they could to neutralize Hastings's home-field advantage.

The Pep Band used an evening dress rehearsal to get ready for the championship game.

Riding on the team bus was like being in the midst of a continuous
pep rally. The cars in the motorcade, decorated with banners and long
blue-and-gold streamers trailing in their wake, would pass our bus and
then let us pass them so they could repeat the maneuver.

Judy Wilkinson's family never missed an away game, and sure
enough, there was her dad's '59 light-green Chrysler on our tail. Right
behind it was Mary McMurtry's family car, with both vehicles packed
with girls prodding the drivers to pull up alongside us.

Watching from inside the bus, someone yelled, "Here they come! Watch out ahead!"

Car horns sounded repeatedly as they passed us, and the girls wildly waved their arms at us and the other cars. It was crazy out there.

As this scene was repeated over and over, I finally moved from my seat on the left-hand side of the bus. I sat in a seat on the other side and closed my eyes to relax. Otherwise, I knew I would be mentally exhausted before we arrived in Hastings.

I thought about how a year ago, Joe di Natalie implored his radio listeners to answer all phone calls with the greeting, "Beat Hastings!" His challenge created such intensity and was so comprehensively picked up by the townspeople, we boys couldn't even go downtown for a haircut without being assailed by the imploring salutations.

This year, Joe made the same call to action, and the result was even more pervasive. Students, teachers, and even neighbors and family members constantly bombarded us with "Beat Hastings!"

I reflected on our other slogan "State by '63!" and involuntarily shook my head at the irony. In basketball, we had the dream and the history of success, and yet failed in our two attempts to even get to the big stage. In football, we had no vision or legacy of achievement. Yet in a colossal surprise we found ourselves one game away from an accomplishment that would have seemed like pure fantasy two years before.

It could have been—*should* have been—"State by '63!" that everyone in town shouted from the rooftops. All but for that damned Holdrege game.

Larry sat down hard next to me and elbowed me. "What's the frown for? Worried about the game?"

"No, I was just thinking about the Holdrege basketball game and our 'State by '63!' pledge. We should have gotten into position where everyone was calling that out to us."

Larry nodded. "I think about it a lot, too, but for different reasons. Maybe we weren't ready. And maybe we needed that loss to make us realize just how much it hurts to let an opportunity like that slip through our fingers.

"I don't know why. But what I do know is with the Gering game, we were given some sort of reprieve. We have a precious chance now at grabbing the brass ring. I am not about to let it go this time."

"Thanks," I said softly. "I agree. I get it. You can count on me."

• • •

We went through our customary pregame ritual. As we were lying on our mats, meditating before putting our pads on, my body felt hyper-alert. Normally I felt my weight going into the mat, but on that day it was like the mat was supporting me, pushing up, almost massaging me.

I was aware of my body as never before. I could move my awareness from my right foot to my left wrist to my right shoulder--anywhere I wanted. Even though my eyes were closed, I could sense my teammates and the situation better than if they were open.

I could tell we were perfectly prepared for the game and were each focused on our individual role within the team. It was the first time I had ever experienced feeling an entire team as being in the zone *before* a game!

Coach Redding ended up doing only one thing different that week, and that was when he added something to his "Payday" mantra that habitually concluded our pregame contemplation.

He quietly told us, "I want to be certain you understand one thing. This game will mean even more to you in the years to come than it does now. You owe it to yourselves to do everything you can, so that win or lose, you will never have any regrets."

We knew *regret*. Holdrege . . . The close call with Gering . . .

He softly closed with, "Boys, you have been given a rare opportunity to compete for the football championship for the great state of Nebraska. Don't cheat yourselves out of this good fortune. You'll never have another chance like this one. Give it everything you've got on every play!"

We quickly suited up. We were impatient to go out on the field and get going.

Finally Coach Redding called us to gather around him.

"Get closer, boys. Put your arms together above me. If we first go on offense, you know our opening series of plays. If we instead start on defense, you know what your roles and assignments are. You're ready. I'm ready. I know you're eager to get out there and mix it up.

"This game belongs to us. Don't let them think for a minute they can take it away from us!" Coach Redding's powerful voice had increased in volume, which signaled he had said his piece.

In unified response, our enthusiastic "Go! Go! Go!" propelled us into the afternoon to fight with Fate again. Did she owe us one, or was coming up short our destiny?

16

Right or Left

Our pregame warm-ups completed, we gathered on our sideline awaiting the coin toss. The Hastings team was still on the field. We were doing lots of anxious shoulder-pad bumping and nervous muttering as we waited.

I saw Larry off by himself, staring down at our empty end zone. I sidled up to him. "What are you thinking, War Horse?" I asked, using an old nickname of mine for him to break the tension, figuring I'd get a laugh or at least a smile in response.

Nothing, except a deep, calming breath. "I'm thinking this has been a crazy journey. My brothers Butch and Kenny came back for the game today, and I'm thinking of all the teams and athletes in all the sports since I started going to their games to watch them play. No one from our school in that time has ever had this chance."

I couldn't think of anything appropriate to say, so I simply stood mute by him, hoping my presence supported him in some way. I knew he must feel a ton of responsibility. I wasn't the star quarterback, I wasn't a co-captain, and I didn't have any brothers present with whom I had shared expectations. And yet I felt his sense of accountability for the result of the game ahead of us.

Pete yelled at Larry, "Wachholtz! They're ready!"

Hastings had cleared the field, and the refs were at the center of the field. It was time for our co-captains to jog out for the coin toss.

Alone with my thoughts, I chewed my mouthpiece fitfully. Football—who would have guessed? Football taught me a lot about myself and my buddies. I learned . . .

From out of nowhere someone grabbed my helmet's face bar and yanked it hard. It was Allan. Jeez . . .

With him pulling my face down to his, I could see his eyes were big with excitement as he spat his words in my face. "C'mon, big guy! Let's get in the game!"

Laughing, I grabbed his helmet with both hands and gave him a big smack with my head and helmet. "Don't worry about me, you crazy guy! What the hell are you doing?"

Allan grinned back. "I'm hoping we go on defense first. I want to go out there and hit someone."

"I agree!" And I did. It was much easier to get mentally into the game on defense.

Watching the coin toss, we saw the refs signal we had first possession. Our fans yelled approvingly.

Allan slapped his hands on his thigh pads and then his hip pads. "So much for that thought. Let's go get 'em."

We ran over to join Larry and Pete as they returned to our sideline, all of us huddling around Coach Redding for the last time before a game.

"What do you have to do out there to win this game, boys?"

We knew the answer. Every one of us called out the response that had been drilled into us.

"Block and tackle!"

"Block and tackle!"

"What do you know how to do better than Hastings?"

"Block and tackle, Coach!"

We crowded closer around him with our arms fully extended upward with hands and fingers seeking one another's.

"Then get your asses out there and prove it!"

"Go! Go! *Go!*"

We received the opening kickoff, and Larry was promptly dropped at our 17-yard line. We felt our way into the game with three straight-

Author's early-game seventy-two yard touchdown pass reception

forward running plays that barely eked out a first down out to the 28-yard line. Another running play, nothing gained.

On the fifth offensive play of the game, Larry called a slant pass to me. I slipped between the defensive coverage, and Larry threw a perfect spiral I caught in full stride about twelve yards downfield. Scooting behind Marv's block right in front of me, I felt like I was running downhill. I didn't stop until I had covered seventy-two yards and crossed the end zone. I could have run forever.

The game was on.

"Way to go, Thomas!"

"First blood!"

The scoreboard read 6–0.

Coach Redding was so impressed by my touchdown, he was speechless. Well, almost. "Thomas! Quit celebrating! You've got work to do right now!"

As we huddled up for our PAT run, I was so excited I couldn't catch my breath. As we broke the huddle, I moved to the right side of the line in our standard overshift. We pushed Hastings's defenders back just enough for Pete to ram the ball over for the extra point.

Now 7–0, our favor. Every point could be critical.

Weber took my kickoff and made a great return to our 42-yard line. I thought we had stopped him two different times, but he escaped both attempts to bring him down.

His first offensive play was a pass into the left flat. Mike made a terrific move on the ball and knocked it away.

They faked us out on their next play, though. Tom Smith took an end-reverse pitch and ran it down to our 8-yard line.

I was surprised. The game was being conducted at a higher speed than I had experienced before. I was going to have to crank my effort up more than I had anticipated.

Punky burst through their line on their next play and stuffed Weber for a seven-yard loss.

"Let's keep moving them back out of field-goal range!"

Uh–oh. Weber tossed a soft pass into the hands of Ken Smith. Touchdown.

Still our favor, 7–6.

"Block the kick!"

Pete and Jerry almost got to it, but Hastings's Doug McArthur sent it through the uprights to tie the game.

Hastings kicked off and stopped Larry on our 20-yard line. We moved the ball to our 42-yard line, largely on a twelve-yard run by Pete up the middle. A deep pass from Larry was intercepted, and Hastings took over on their 35.

Two plays later, Punky crashed though their line again, creating and covering a handoff fumble on their 38.

"Good going, Punky!"

I was sure glad we had him creating havoc in the middle this year.

We toughed out a first down to their 27. In the huddle, Larry called a motion-misdirect pass play to Rodger, a maneuver that had never failed to gain us some good yardage. Rodger's eyes lit up.

Twenty-seven yards later, we were congratulating Rodger for his touchdown reception at a critical time. We needed that score.

With the scoreboard reading 13–7, everyone in the stadium knew what the next call would be. They knew we would make a line over-shift and hand the ball off to Pete.

We didn't fool anyone anymore with our point-after overshift. Defenses stacked their biggest and toughest players opposite us in every slot and dared us to take them on.

We took the dare and won the battle one more time. Pete finished the job and captured another precious point.

We led 14–7.

After effective defensive series by both teams, the first half ended with the scoreboard showing North Platte Bulldogs–14, Hastings Tigers–7.

Coach Redding's halftime conversation was a surprising low-key recounting of successes and shortcomings. For a change, there was no criticism of our effort or courage displayed. We had apparently met his expectations.

Coach Redding polished off our final high-school football halftime chalk talk.

"I'm proud of how you've responded in the first half, but you still have the more important half ahead of you. Before we go back out there, I want you to turn to one another and look each other directly in the eyes. Right now. Go ahead, get eye to eye.

"Commit to that person you will not let him down. He's the one you're playing for. He's your teammate, and he's put in a year's hard labor and now needs you to go nonstop with him for twenty more minutes. He has no one else to count on but you."

He paused to let us silently and solemnly complete his assigned task. I had goose bumps all over. I was so jacked, I thought I'd explode.

Coach gathered us around him again, this time more paternally than as a coach. We held our hands high and pressed our arms in toward the middle over him. He smiled and quietly said, "OK, let's go finish this thing."

For me, the personal commitment to maximum effort came easy. Having suffered through the devastating basketball season-ending loss last year to Holdrege and nearly encountering a similar emotional football-related fate against Gering a week before, I agreed with Larry. I was not about to let that happen to our team and me again. I was confident everyone else on the team felt exactly the same way.

Hastings wanted our lifeblood. They couldn't have it.

But after Weber returned my second-half opening kickoff 55 yards, I wished someone had told him that.

"Stiffen up, you guys!"

Ten hard-fought plays later, Hastings was at our 3-yard line. We had done it before. We needed to hold them there and get the momentum back.

Dammit. They jammed it across our goal line.

It was 14–13, barely in our favor.

Coach called time out and motioned us all to the sideline.

"Settle down, you guys! We need to block this kick, or we'll have a mess on our hands. Here's what I want you to do. Instead of lining up in the slots as usual, I want you linemen to line up directly on their players. Nose to nose. I want your snot blowing out on their faces.

"You linebackers, I want you to line up behind our linemen. Put your hands right on their asses. When the ball is snapped, the linemen will go through the slot to the right and the linebackers through the slot to the left. Linemen right, linebackers left. Got it?"

We nodded obediently.

"They won't know what hit 'em. Just meet up together at the ball. Hell, you may all get through."

As we lined up in our new formation, I saw the surprise in the Hastings players' eyes as they searched for the appropriate blocking assignments. Before they resolved their confusion, the ball was snapped.

As MacArthur stepped into his second PAT kick, everyone on our team gave an extra effort, an added surge, and four of us broke through with a good shot at blocking it.

Allan's critical block of Hastings's point-after kick

One of our hands was at the right place at the right time. Its out-stretched fingers caught the ball squarely in midflight.

But the player who got to the kick had no idea whether it was his right hand or left, as the hand belonged to Allan. He didn't even know whether he went through the left or right slot.

We didn't care.

"Way to go, Allan!"

In a season-long important supporting role, away from the glare of publicity, the kid with dyslexia had continually validated Coach Redding's assessment that "Allan has done more with his talent than anyone I have ever coached." Allan preferred not having center-stage exposure, but the flickering spotlight was starting to focus its beam on him.

Ahead 14–13 with seventeen minutes to go. It seemed an eternity.

That blocked kick was just what we needed in more ways than one. Stopping Hastings from tying us reenergized us completely. We thrust-and-parried the rest of the third quarter.

As the fourth quarter started, we controlled the ball deep in our own territory and were still holding on to our one-point lead.

Ten excruciatingly long minutes to go.

Couldn't think about what it would mean to win. Couldn't think about anything except block and tackle, block and tackle.

Crap, Hastings intercepted on our 38.

"Let's bear down *now*, guys!"

Bending, we yielded yardage grudgingly, but they pushed persistently to our 8-yard line to gain a first down.

On the next play, Mike made a perfect spin-move around his man and into their backfield, dropping Weber for a seven-yard loss.

"What an effort, Mike!"

Weber decided running the ball deep in our territory wasn't going to work, so he threw two passes in a row. Both misfired. Fourth down.

Deciding against a field goal, he tried another pass, but Larry batted it down. We took over on downs.

We moved the line of scrimmage a few yards but had to punt on fourth down. Ozzie made an uncharacteristically poor snap along the ground. Larry barely gathered it up, and his hurried kick traveled only to our 39-yard line.

Hastings took over again. Weber hit Norris for a quick pass that moved them down to our 22-yard line. We all shouted encouragement to each other to hold them again. Kirkman and Reuter decided to do better than that and pulled Weber down for a five-yard loss. Mike was in there again.

Two missed passes later, Hastings decided with only 2:58 left on the clock, they had better try a field goal. We lined up the same way as when we blocked their last attempt. McArthur launched the ball with his foot, but with Pete bearing down on him, he had to hurry and pulled it way left.

Whew!

"Let's hold on to the ball and run the clock out!"

Only 2:52 left.

"We can do it."

No, we couldn't.

Three plays, little yardage gained. We had to punt again.

"C'mon, Ozzie!"

Ozzie nailed the snap, and Larry pounded a forty-seven-yarder toward the sidelines that came to rest on Hastings's 28-yard line.

Weber right away sent shock waves through our bodies, though, with a long pass to Tom Smith who ran to our 43-yard line.

Marv and I kept pinching in from our end positions. Along with intense inside pressure and deep, blanket-like coverage, we forced Weber into four straight hurried passes that all missed their intended mark. We took over on downs yet again.

Only 1:36 left. *Now* we could hold on to the ball and run the clock down.

You could see the despair in the Hastings players' eyes as they realized the same situation. The game was in the bag for us.

"Oh, God, are you kidding me?"

Hastings had forced a fumble on our 47-yard line. They had yet another chance, with 1:11 left to play.

I had seen something like this in a hockey game on TV, when a team lost two players to the penalty box. Their opponent swarmed through their shorthanded lineup, firing shot after shot at the goalie. We were just like that poor sonuvabitch goalie.

We needed to adjust our pads and jocks. We couldn't keep giving this team more chances to beat us. We couldn't keep giving Weber more opportunities to steal this game from us.

We were going to see nothing but passes for certain. "Rush Weber hard, guys!"

Weber came out throwing, as expected. His first pass was thrown over my head toward Ken Smith. Allan knocked it down.

Weber got his second pass off just as I put my hands on him. I released him in frustration at getting there late and turned to watch his throw sail deep down the middle of the field toward Tom Smith.

"Somebody knock it away!"

Instead, Rodger decided the ball belonged to him. Snatching it from Smith's extended hands, Rodger hauled in the fickle pigskin and clamped it close to his body, wrapping both arms tightly around his prized possession. Running behind grateful blocks from the rest of us, he wound his interception return through hurtling bodies all the way to Hastings's 12-yard line.

It was the most beautiful interception in the world. Ever.

We didn't dare assume anything this time. Even though there were fewer than forty seconds in the game and Hastings had no timeouts left, we needed to take it step by step.

"One play at a time."

As we had seen, anything could happen.

"Hold on to the ball!"

17

Boys to Men

Twenty . . . Nineteen . . . Eighteen . . . The seconds ticked off the clock.

Hastings was out of timeouts. We didn't have to snap the ball again. The game, the victory, the state championship were all ours.

Ozzie, then Rich, and then the rest of us unbuckled our chinstraps to remove our helmets. We elbowed each other in excitement and anticipation.

Fifteen . . . Fourteen . . . Thirteen . . .

My eyes watered as I saw the Hastings players cross the now defunct line of scrimmage to congratulate us. Wayne Weber sought me out. "I'm going to be seeing you in my dreams chase me all over the field!"

Tom Smith passed by, and I offered up "Great game!" but he was intent on getting off the field before the game officially ended. I sympathized with him not wanting to get caught up in the joyous bedlam of our supporters gathering on our sideline, which, like a storm brewing on the western horizon, would soon be upon us.

Eight . . . Seven . . . Six . . .

Pete grabbed and pulled me into a hastily formed huddle with the rest of our team. Eleven heads down but with eyebrows up, our eyes searched out each other's affirmation. Every part of my body ached, but it was a good hurt.

Sweat drops fell. I could taste the salt. I could feel the beating of my heart. I heard the heavy breathing of my teammates, shoulder pads to shoulder pads. I glanced from one friend to another in growing exhilaration. I dropped my helmet on the ground and embraced my teammates on either side in one final, private effort to make this moment last.

"Way to go!"

"We did it!"

"I can't believe it!"

Three . . . Two . . . One . . .

I heard the game-ending whistle.

"Look out!"

Postgame celebration of our 1962 Nebraska state championship victory

The referee had sprinted into the path of the oncoming rush of people to hand the game ball to Coach Redding, who was being swept along by the crowd. Like a flash flood suddenly encountering an obstacle in its thundering path, the group momentarily slowed around our oblivious coach and the flinching referee as the ball and congratulations were quickly accepted.

What I saw looked like slow motion and fast forward at the same time. The dynamic mass could not stop its momentum and spilled awkwardly around the pair, gathering speed again toward us. I could make out faces in one sense, and yet the group seemed as one to me.

I picked up my helmet just as the throng hit us and burst us apart like an explosion within our huddle.

Our teammates from the sidelines were the first to reach us to join in the brotherhood of celebration, throwing punches to my body and harshly rubbing my crewcut.

"Ouch!"

"Way to go, Jerry!"

"Good job, Bruce!"

"We did it, Jack!"

"Jim, can you believe this?"

Fighting their way between us boys, the cheerleaders and other girls reached us. Nice, big, wet kisses—that was more like it! I got kissed from both sides as someone reached between them from behind to give me a hug around the waist. She wouldn't let go.

The girls sure smelled good. I felt like a knight in shining armor that just saved the castle's maidens from a killer dragon. I bet I was blushing a hundred shades of red. I didn't want it to end.

Over the heads of the girls, I saw a group of men approaching. They were smartly dressed in suits and ties, overcoats and dress hats. A mixture of players' fathers and local businessmen, the men reached in through the collection of girls to grab my right hand for handshakes, and the girls respectfully moved aside.

"Congratulations!"

"Great job!"

"You had us scared up there in the stands!"

"You've done the town proud!"

There were slaps to my shoulders and taps on my head. It was hard to describe the feeling evoked by having adult males give me that kind of recognition. It was akin to a tribal rite of passage. I soaked it up.

As they moved on, I noticed the people circling from player to player were all talking at once and gesturing like crazy. Everyone was having a blast.

But where was Coach Redding? I looked around from group to group but didn't see him. Suddenly he materialized at my side.

"Coach! There you are! We did it, Coach!"

He grabbed my right hand with his right hand and my upper right arm with his left hand. He pulled me into a hug. "Great game, Bob," he called out over the din. "You came through just like I knew you would. I'm proud of you. I'm so happy for all of you!"

I wanted to tell him how great it felt to be hugged by him and to get his approval and how happy I was we had won it all for him. But before any sounds came out of my open mouth, Coach Redding disappeared again, swallowed up by the churning mass.

Wham!

I damn near fell down as someone ran hard into me from the side. It was Larry, grinning from ear to ear. "Way to go, you big horse. I always told you, you should go out for football!"

I grabbed his shoulder pads and shook them. "You never told me it would be this much fun!" Before I could say anything else, another bunch of classmates swarmed us, wrestling with us and bouncing us around like big blowup dolls.

They released me long enough so I could greet my parents. My folks looked like they wanted to join in with us but were afraid of being trampled. Rightfully so, as seconds later another wave of students in band and Pep Club uniforms overwhelmed us. My parents backpedaled to safety, proudly waving at Larry and me as they left the on-field celebrations to us youngsters.

The pandemonium continued.

"Congratulations!"

"You guys are the best ever!"

"I can't believe how you kept giving them the ball in the last quarter but still held them scoreless."

I responded, "Thanks! I know. I can't believe it, either."

I received and repeated the same sentiments time and again, finally making it back to the locker room, only to have the festivities start all over again. Half of North Platte must have been in there.

I had never seen anything like it. Teachers and bankers and parents were all acting like children opening Christmas packages. With their hair and clothes and hats all in disarray, everyone looked like they had been out on the field with us.

I caught up with Pete, who was horsing around with Mike and Rich in a corner of the room. "Great game, you guys. Can you believe it?"

Coach Redding
is congratulated
by Hastings's
Coach Ollie
Smith.

Pete had a smile a mile wide. "No! That was something out there. They kept coming and coming at us."

Larry lunged in and gave Pete a giant bear hug, and they wordlessly acknowledged their accomplishments and leadership on the field. Our two stars had more than stepped up to the challenge, and they deserved to share their appreciation of each other.

I moved around the locker room, from cluster to cluster. "Hello, Mr. Wachholtz. Larry played a terrific game. I bet Butch and Kenny enjoyed it."

"Mr. Tuenge, that was some interception by Rodger, wasn't it?"

"Thanks for that block, Marv!"

"Punky, you were *living* in their backfield all afternoon!"

"Allan, what have you got to say for yourself now? Thanks for that blocked kick."

Coach Redding finally called for a break in the melee. "Hello! Hello, everyone!"

As the noise level fell enough for him to be heard, he stood on one of the benches on the side of the room so everyone could see his beaming face.

He looked like he had been in battle, too. We definitely had not made it easy on him the last quarter. He must have wondered what the hell we were doing at times.

But at that moment he looked to me just like the young Crump Redding he described as having fought all of the boys in each new school he attended and again coming out on top.

"Thanks to all of you who made the trip down here to Hastings. Your support all season long has been outstanding. You have made my family's first two years in North Platte fun and rewarding, and I'm glad we could return the favor!"

The eclectic collection responded with loud hand-clapping and foot-stomping.

Crump motioned for quiet. "Now, I want to talk to my boys.

"No, that's wrong. You're no longer boys! You've become men before our very eyes, and you deserve every honor you'll receive from this game and this season. In just two short years, you made the investment I promised would yield a winner. You made the sacrifices of your personal time away from the practice field to lift weights and stay in shape—sacrifices necessary if we were going to turn North Platte into the powerhouse we deserved to be."

My heart beat faster as the crowd started cheering.

"Congratulations to you, men," Coach continued. "I'm proud to have been a part of this with you! From the bottom of my heart, thank you!"

As everyone cheered louder and clapped as hard as they could, my eyes teared up. The shouting and applause turned into a thunderous, rhythmic version of our pregame chant.

"Go! Go! *Go!*"

Coach Redding hopped off the bench and shooed people outside so we could finally get to our showers. Taking my shoulder pads off, I watched as he received congratulations from Superintendent Otto Oakes and the school board president, Harold Kay.

Then, to my surprise, I saw Gregg McBride squeeze in through the people leaving and walk up to Coach Redding. On my way to the showers, I couldn't hear what they were saying, but Coach Redding looked happy, excited, and animated as McBride vigorously shook his hand.

With the townspeople gone, the locker room was still except for the sound of the showers. I could have stood there forever. The hot water felt like it was washing me clear down to my bones.

We dressed in silence, having already spent our vocal energy.

As we exited the visiting team's locker room, the last shred of daylight was about to dissipate. I had expected everyone to have already left for North Platte before it got too dark. But it seemed most of our supporters were still there, including the band, which started playing the moment we came out of the building. My throat constricted at the sound of the music and rhythmic beat of the snare and bass drums.

After receiving repeated warm expressions of appreciation from friends and relatives, we finally boarded our bus. It pulled slowly away through the crowd. They didn't want us to go, and we didn't want to leave them.

But I knew they would have a lot of fun on the way home, especially all those who were taking the train back to North Platte. It would be crazy aboard that train.

As our bus left the school grounds and all of the commotion behind, we sat back and quietly relaxed, alone with our individual thoughts.

We had done it.

We had achieved what we dared to start dreaming about—the 1962 Nebraska State Football Championship.

Coach Redding had his second state championship in two different states, and we had a memory for a lifetime. We had cashed the biggest paycheck of all.

Someone on the team had always been in position to do what was needed when the opportunity presented itself or the situation required it. That may have been what it took to win it all.

Plus, we won the title with a perfect record. Every year there would always be one team that would win the title, but winning it with an undefeated season was a rarity, and I knew that unique accomplishment would forever be precious to us.

● ● ●

Gradually, a complete release of the game's pressure and postgame revelry was reflected in everyone's increasingly smiling faces and sparkling eyes. Before long, the bus was filled with the harmony of cheers and yells and recollections of great plays and efforts "above and beyond." The interplay between us became so boisterous, our journey to our dinner location seemed to go by in a flash.

After every sporting event east of North Platte, we stopped for dinner in Lexington on our way home. In Lexington was a family-owned restaurant named Hagedon's, which we had adopted as our own. They spoiled us with great quantities of food, and we were not embarrassed at all by our gluttonous intake of their featured entree of fried chicken, mashed potatoes, and chicken gravy, finished off with cake and ice cream with chocolate sauce.

It was good we had worked up an appetite, because we were headed to a feast. In honor of our victory, the owner and staff went overboard serving us extra food plus as many helpings of dessert as we could force down. They had as much fun as we did, with all of us keeping it barely civilized enough to stay this side of a food fight.

After stuffing ourselves beyond reason, we clamored back on the bus for the final leg of our journey home.

Coach Redding was not making the trip with us. He and a few boosters left ahead of us to go to Lawrence, Kansas, to watch the Kansas-Nebraska college football game the next day. We figured he would be getting quite a reception from his old friend, Kansas Coach Jack Mitchell. He deserved it.

The other coaches and Max rode up front, where Coach usually sat. The night was dark and cool, the bus was warm, and our stomachs were bursting. Soon we were all sprawled out in the blissful slumber of the young and innocent—and victorious.

18

End

"Hey, Max. Wake up!" The driver's voice jolted me awake. He was alarmed about something.

"Look up ahead! There, in the dark!" he called out to our trainer.

Sitting behind Max, I became immediately alert.

"Where are we?" someone asked the driver.

"Only a few miles east of North Platte," he replied, anxiety in his voice. "We're almost home."

He pumped the brakes. The coaches in the other front-row seats woke up as the bus slowed.

I squinted, trying to discern what the problem was.

"Max, this looks like one helluva accident," Coach Johnson assessed.

I silently agreed as I made out the shapes of automobiles in the moonlight, strewn alongside the highway.

"My God . . ." mumbled Max.

Leaning over the back of his seat, my mind raced back to earlier in the season when our team trip had to detour around a traffic fatality in this same general area. But where that had been a one-car accident, this apparently was a pileup of huge proportions.

Concerned awareness spread through the bus.

"Wake up!"

"What happened?"

It was as if a low-voltage current had been connected to all my teammates, with our apprehension at the front of the bus steadily flowing from front to back, awakening the passengers row by row. Everyone on both sides pressed their faces against the windows for a better look.

It became silent, as if all sound had been sucked out of the bus. I figured everyone was just like me, hoping their friends and loved ones had made it home safe and sound and weren't part of this apparent carnage.

Larry and Pete moved up the aisle from the back where they had commandeered the rear seat, to check things out. As they reached where I was sitting, my eyes caught theirs as I grimaced and shook my head with worry.

Larry stepped forward, next to the driver, and sat on the floor with his feet on the steps, looking out intently through the massive windshield. Pete stood next to me, holding Max's seatback as he bent forward to see better.

After a few minutes of concerned observation, Larry murmured, "I don't think this is an accident."

Once our bus had slowed to a crawl, I could see what he meant. There was more order than disorder to the array of countless vehicles. The cars and trucks, all with their lights off, seemed to my night-adjusted eyesight to be aligned side-by-side along the highway's angled shoulders, facing up and in toward the highway from both sides.

Suddenly, as if on cue, all of the headlights turned on. The beams lifted up and across the highway as if they were crossed sabers held high in a military ceremony. Horns started honking at the same time.

Larry turned around to look at me with amazement on his face, exclaiming, "Wow!"

Pete stood up and grabbed my shoulder, but I couldn't take my eyes off the scene outside. What had just minutes before been a black, mind-crushing silence turned into a white-light, ear-pounding symphony.

Reality finally dawned. Hundreds of our fans and supporters had been organized to form an enormous welcoming committee, waiting hours in the cold and dark for us to come rolling back into town after midnight.

Lights flashing and siren wailing, a police car pulled in front of the bus. The officer stuck his left arm out his window and signaled us to follow. All of the vehicles pulled in one-by-one behind us.

As the huge caravan followed us into town, we wound our way through several residential streets as people spilled out of their houses onto their lawns with makeshift victory signs, brooms, or whatever else they could find to wave.

Despite the late hour, it seemed like everyone in town knew what had happened and needed to be part of the celebration. The capper was one elderly gentleman wrapped in a blanket against the cold who struggled to his feet from his rocker on his front porch. Gathering himself on his crutches, he leaned onto one and raised the other in salute. My eyes watered as I watched several players wave back to him.

We were humbled and overcome with the massive display of collective town spirit. A reservoir dam of emotion had split open, with all of the sentiment rushing at us. Who could even breathe? It was impossible to take it all in.

Tears streamed down our faces. We supposed tough guys had no defenses left to stem the tide of grateful appreciation for what the townspeople had done. As I looked back throughout the bus, the streetlights and vehicle headlights and taillights reflected off wet grinning faces and saucer-sized eyes.

When we arrived at the parking lot next to our high school locker room, the cheerleaders and much of the Pep Band and Pep Club were waiting for us. I wondered how long they had been there. As the rest of our supportive caravan pulled in around the school and unloaded, I guessed there were several hundred people attending the impromptu pep rally.

The gathering mixed and mingled, not wanting the night to end.

After a while, I needed a breather, so I moved away from the crowd. I saw Larry and Pete leaning on the fender of a car, so I headed over there to see what they were up to. Winding my way there, I saw Rich join them and put his right foot up on the front bumper.

I greeted them. "Hey, guys, whatcha doin'? Unbelievable what the town and school did for us tonight. What a surprise!"

"That's just what we were talking about," Larry said. "I wish Coach could have been here with us on the bus ride home and now for this celebration."

Pete nodded vigorously. "He missed something special. But I heard a welcoming party is being organized for his return. We'll be doing this all over again out at the airport Sunday night."

Mike and Allan had joined us, with Mike contributing, "Great. I miss him here tonight."

Allan added, "It will be terrific to watch his reaction when he sees for himself what this is like. It'll be some show."

After Marv and Rodney also came over, Larry grinned and announced to the expanding audience, "I have even bigger news. Harold Rasmussen told me he's going to have the whole team out to his bowling alley this week for an all-you-can-eat banquet of Kentucky Fried Chicken."

"All right! I love the Cedar Bowl."

"I love Kentucky Fried Chicken!"

"Good for Mr. Rasmussen!"

"He'll be sorry! He's never seen the way you eat."

Most of our team had made their way to gather around our two co-captains. In the chilly night air, everyone's breath was coming out in small vapor clouds. From where I was standing, my teammates' crew-cuts and flattops were backlit by the school's security lights, obscuring their faces. What a picture it made. I wished I could somehow capture that image.

We slowly joined back in with the others. Parents and players hugged, players and girlfriends kissed and held each other tight, and everyone stayed on until all emotion was finally spent.

Eventually there was nothing more to do but go home.

Larry walked over to tell me he asked his parents to take him to the hospital to check out the soreness in his ribs. He suspected a few of them were cracked. He had not said a word about it before.

"Good night, Mr. and Mrs. Wachholtz. Take good care of him. Good luck, Larry. What a day and night, huh?"

"See you, Big Bob. We did it! Sleep well."

Pete drove up in his '57 Studebaker Commander, music blaring, to say goodnight.

"What's that, Pete? KOMA out of Oklahoma City?"

"Yup! You guys have a great night. Congratulations again!"

"You, too. Great game!" I yelled as Pete whisked off into the night with Trisha and friends.

I saw Marv departing with Jim Huffman and their girlfriends in Jim's car. Mike and Rich and Lowell Harvey were leaving together. Hardly anyone remained, so I knew it was time to go.

Allan and I left together on foot. After a few blocks, we parted and went our separate ways. I took my time walking the few remaining blocks home in the dark, enjoying being alone with my thoughts and fresh memories. I had walked this same route countless times, but it was my first time as a state champion.

When I got home, the excitement picked up all over again. My parents and sister and I hugged and interrupted each other with questions and comments about the game and the town's overpowering welcome-home celebration. Mom fixed me some snacks, and I appreciatively munched on them as we relived the events of the day.

Finally it was time to go upstairs and collapse into bed, with my last thoughts before falling asleep being, "What a day. What a night. There can never be anything that will top this."

In the deepest part of my exhausted and dream-filled sleep, I reluctantly became aware someone was knocking on the front door downstairs. I hoped my parents would answer it, which they eventually did. I heard the front door open, then a brief conversation I couldn't make out, followed by Mom's request, "Bob, can you come downstairs?"

When I got to the bottom of the stairs, a man I didn't recognize was waiting. My mom and dad didn't introduce me to him, so I assumed he was unfamiliar to them, too.

He didn't give his name, but he had a big smile on his face as he spoke. "Sorry again for waking you folks up, but congratulations, Bob, on a great game. Since you played end, I wanted you to have this."

With that, he handed me a bundle of something wrapped in newspapers, then said a quick goodbye and was gone. The package was surprisingly heavy for its size.

I ripped off the paper to discover a slice of large-bore cast-iron pipe covered with layers of peeling white paint. It was about twelve inches long. My initial feeling was one of frustration at being awoken for a practical joke of an old, mangled piece of pipe.

Then the handwriting on the chipped paint leapt out at me.

The end of the goalpost
for the end of the team!

Author's "end" of the goalpost

Epilogue

Immediately following our high-school state championship football season, Larry, Pete, and I were awarded All-State honors as well as selected for the annual summer Shrine Game that honored seniors from all schools across the state. Mike, Punky, Allan, Jerry, and Ozzie received well-earned all-conference honors from numerous sports-writers, while Mike and Allan received specific recognition awards for their play in the championship game.

In the days and weeks that followed, team members gained several pounds each as a result of numerous celebratory luncheons and banquets held on our behalf.

In the midst of those 1962 postseason football-related distractions, we launched our final run at our youthful basketball dream of "State By '63!" and carved out only a modest regular season record of eleven wins against five losses. However, after being beaten twice by McCook during the season, we pulled off a District-tournament upset of our own against them to finally "make it to state."

Unfortunately, we were knocked out of the competition in the first round by a much stronger team from the Omaha area. Thank goodness our football success trumped our Pledge failure.

After high school, Larry and Pete both became football standouts at the University of Nebraska. Their football fans in North Platte were thus given a euphoric four-year bonus by being allowed to become an

Top: Postseason celebration at Harold Rasmussen's Cedar Bowl; author at head of table—to my left are Punky, Larry, Pete, Jay Welden (standing), Bruce Kuhlmann, Marv, Ozzie, and Rich; to my right are Rodney and Rodger; *Bottom:* North Platte's 1962 state championship team's coaches and players seated along sidelines of late-season University of Nebraska football game at Lincoln

The University of Nebraska's North Platte contingent: Pete and Larry hold aloft the 1966–1967 "N Club Sweetheart," Trisha.

intimate part of Cornhusker football. In their sophomore and junior years, Nebraska-mania reached a fever pitch as each year the team played in a postseason bowl game for the national title.

And in their senior year together at Nebraska, Trisha Bystrom gave the school's sports scene a further North Platte flair when a majority of all varsity athletes voted her to the coveted annual N Club Sweetheart honor.

Larry had left behind an incredible high-school legacy across all sports for others to chase, becoming a member of the Nebraska High School Sports Hall of Fame. At Nebraska, his broad athletic gifts were on display as he won All-University intramural titles in racquetball and badminton, and was named to the All-University intramural basketball team for three years, during which his fraternity team won the university basketball championship each year.

But it was on the prestigious varsity football field where he really shone. After starting three years as a defensive back, during which he rewrote the record books for interceptions, punt and kick-off return yardage, and scoring (including his kicking PATs and field goals), Larry was recognized with consensus All-American honors in his senior year. He also won dual Nebraska-team honors of being elected co-captain and voted the Tom Novak Award for outstanding senior.

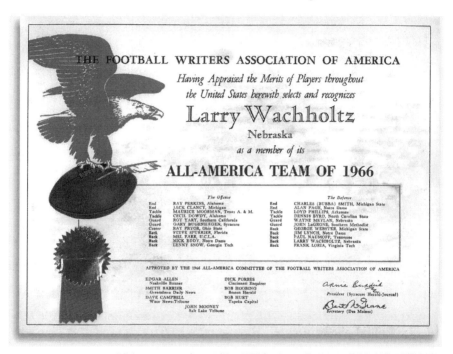

Larry's All-American certificates

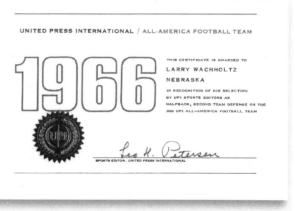

Years later Larry was named by the *Omaha World-Herald* to an all-time university team and inducted into the celebrated Nebraska University Football Hall of Fame, securing his place in the school's history.

During the spring of 1963, as Pete contemplated his future after high school, he discovered he had become a nationally top-rated football prospect when he began being courted by many of the big Division I schools. That was no surprise to the rest of us, as we knew Pete possessed the prototypical football physique, demeanor, and skills sought by their football programs.

Local boosters and the Nebraska coaching staff eventually persuaded Pete to go to Nebraska, where Coach Redding predicted he would become a defensive standout. Coach Redding and Pete were

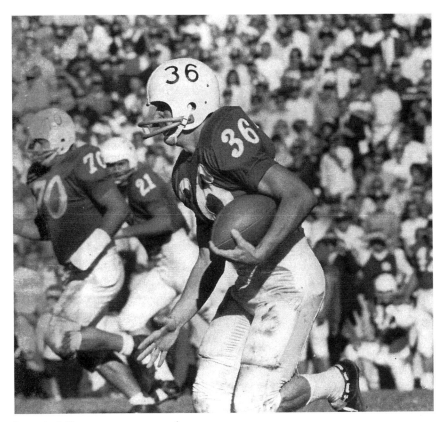

Larry (#36), returns intercepted pass.

Pete (#48), running over Big Eight foes

both surprised when Pete was instead assigned to the offense. However, Pete quickly earned the reputation from the offensive backfield coaches as being the best blocking fullback they had ever worked with.

His remarkable abilities were further recognized by the Minnesota Vikings of professional football, who drafted him out of college to play for their team.

None of our team's success nor Larry's and Pete's collegiate achievements would have happened, though, without the man we now refer to as "Crump," although in person he was always "Coach Redding." We credit George Crump Redding with all we achieved then and for much of who we are today. Nearly fifty years since that championship game, we teammates universally feel tremendous gratitude for him.

I know his impact on my life was immeasurable. After high school, I entered the US Air Force Academy, and many times all the

Left: Pete (#33), with Minnesota Vikings against New York Giants; *Below:* North Platte fans greet Crump at airport to celebrate state championship with him.

way through graduation I silently thanked Crump for toughening me up. Throughout my subsequent corporate-career success, I regularly voiced the same credit to anyone who would listen.

Doing the research for this book gave me the opportunity to meet with Crump and finally thank him personally for his mentorship. A grown man by then, I still felt in his presence like a young athlete on the practice field waiting for his approval.

His amazing recall of players and events after forty years surprised me, but what stood out most for me was how proud he was of being able to finish his coaching career in North Platte—fulfilling his commitment to stay in one place until all his children graduated from high school.

Our time together was a constant reminder of how he had stirred, ignited, and yanked something out of all of us, yet left us with much more than we gave. We had learned and practiced his values as he embraced and taught them, unaware they had become ours for life:

By keeping things simple, our entire team had clarity and was able to focus on our objectives.

By repeating fundamentals until they became second nature, we reduced our mistakes, created opportunities, and became capable of beating teams on the basics alone.

By working hard without boundaries, we built stamina to outlast our competition.

By accepting accountability for our efforts, we constantly improved to become the best we could be.

Crump only recently passed away, which caused me to reflect upon how brief our interaction was. He was directly involved in our lives for only a few months of each of two years. He had to work with the hand he was dealt. He wasn't able to change anything that happened before his arrival to lessen or facilitate his task. He wasn't able to create more time in which to do his work. For our brief encounter with him to have produced such a burst of personal and team accomplishment was remarkable.

At the time, people labeled our buying into Crump and his style of leadership as "teamwork." But it was more than that.

Over my life, I've seen productive collaborations occur in assorted group activities, including sports, music, and business. That's teamwork.

At its best, though, when all members of an organization come together like we did in 1962 to form a *passionate, learned, fully invested, soul-sourced and soul-stirring orchestration of wills,* that's magic.

● ● ●

My research provided numerous humorous vignettes that never made it into this story, but following is one that deserves a place.

Merle Bauer, the clever Holdrege basketball coach who engineered their devastating upset of our team in 1962 to keep us out of the state tournament, several years later became North Platte Public Schools' Director of Athletics. Shortly after Bauer moved his family to North Platte, he needed some dental work. In a fitting piece of synchronicity, he thumbed through the phone book and noticed a familiar name.

Bauer called and made an appointment. After he was seated in the dentist's chair, the dentist, holding a drill in one hand and a dentist's pick in the other, said to him only half-facetiously, "I would have thought I would be the last person you would permit near your mouth with sharp instruments!"

Bauer laughed, and said, "Dr. States, I can't believe you still remember that game!"

Jim States answered with a wry smile, "If you only knew . . ."

● ● ●

For my final follow-up to our team's story, I hoped during my research to learn the identity of the man who delivered the unique package of the goalpost section to me the night of the championship game. To my surprise, no coach or other player had been visited, so his identity remains a mystery.

Over the years, through many household moves back and forth across the country, I somehow managed to lose several pieces of sentimental sports and business memorabilia.

But . . .

I still have that weighty and treasured mangled piece of pipe from that magical night in 1962.

Opposite side of author's goalpost section: "Beat Hastings"

Tribute

To the NPHS Bulldog football teams of 1961 and 1962, with apologies to those left out of the story or short-changed in their reported contributions. Coach Redding would not have approved of any such omissions.

1962: State Champions; Big Ten Champions; West Division Champions; Perfect Season: 9–0
Left to right: Top: Coach Johnson, Jerry James, Jim Schwartz, Bob Oswald, Jack Edwards, Bob Thomas, Jim Huffman, Pete Tatman, Nathan Miller, Alan Dowhower, Don Abegg; *Middle:* Coach Folsom, Jim Howard, Jim Dahlgren, Bob Roberts, Rick Sorenson, Dennis Raetz, Bill Brown, Dick McWilliams, Pete Nielson, Terry Whitesel, Terry Hunt, Coach Redding; *Bottom:* Herb von Goetz, Rich Graham, Larry Wachholtz, Lowell Harvey, Art Pacheco, Herb Weichman, Marv Binegar, Rodger Tuenge, Bob Reuter, Rodney Tuenge, Allan Whitesel, Mike Kirkman, Steve Van Cleave

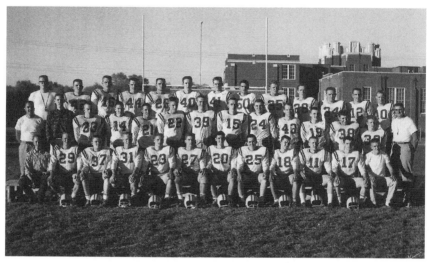

1961: Big Ten Champions; West Division Champions; Season Record: 6–2–2

Left to right: Top: Coach Best, Dennis Gilbert, Gene Jones, Gary Scheet, Denny Lienemann, Bill Stephenson, Denny Nelson, Dick Bockus, Gary Sexson, Larry Nelson, Dave Nichols, Terry Timmerman, Jim Kubicek; *Middle:* Coach Folsom, Bob Maline, Melvin Prickett, Galen Skinner, Duane Andre, Jim Huffman, Bob Thomas, Jack Edwards, Bob Oswald, Bruce Tuttle, Byron Boslau, Jim Lantis, Don Titus, Coach Redding; *Bottom:* Steve Van Cleave, Rodney Tuenge, Bob Reuter, Rodger Tuenge, Allan Whitesel, Pete Tatman, Marv Binegar, Jerry James, Mike Kirkman, Larry Wachholtz, Art Pacheco, Tom Wisdom

Endorsements

Reading Bob Thomas's book *CRUMP* brought back many memories of growing up in a mid-sized town in Nebraska in the 1950s. Those of us interested in athletics played practically every sport and started out in our elementary school years, playing pickup games every night after school. We all envisioned ourselves as being great athletes and had big dreams. This was true of a group of young men living in North Platte, Nebraska, in the late fifties and early sixties. The story of how George (Crump) Redding galvanized this group of young men into a great football team and how he coordinated their drive, ambition, and their visions of greatness into an outstanding state championship football team is truly worth reading. I knew Crump and had his son Dave play for me at the University of Nebraska and knew that he had exceptional leadership ability. I feel that the book is an excellent profile in the difference that leadership makes. I recommend the book, as it not only chronicles the story of an excellent football team but also discusses its two star players, Larry Wachholtz and Pete Tatman, who later became great players at the University of Nebraska in the 1960s.

Tom Osborne
Athletic Director

University of Nebraska

We brothers have had the opportunity to read Bob's book about the North Platte 1962 State Championship team. Actually, we both immediately read it a second time. It took us back to those times in North Platte when football was on everyone's mind.

For Dave, it was watching Crump (our dad) through the eyes of a kid in the fifth grade, dreaming of the day when he could suit up with the big boys. For Clark, a sophomore at the time, it was reliving being around a group of upperclassmen he knew and idolized, wanting to be a part of their elite group.

We both agree it was a unique situation—a perfect combination of exceptional young men and a coach with the right set of motivational skills. The resulting championship would have been impossible for one without the other.

Bob, you nailed it.

Clark and Dave Redding

About the Author

Bob Thomas carried his coach's lessons and the power of teamwork to college, the military, and corporate executive positions. He has been the President and CEO of Nissan Motor Corporation, USA, and COO of Edmunds.com, Inc. He resides with his wife in Hawaii.

Image Credits

Page

154, 155	*Telegraph-Bulletin*
158	*Telegraph-Bulletin*
168	Courtesy Bob Thomas
170 top	Unknown; courtesy Butch Rasmussen
170 bottom	Unknown; courtesy Clark Redding
171	Unknown; courtesy Trisha Bystrom Trowbridge
172 both	Courtesy Larry Wachholtz
173	Unknown, courtesy Larry Wachholtz
174	Unknown, courtesy Pete Tatman
175 top	Unknown, courtesy Pete Tatman
175 bottom	Unknown; source: school annual
178	Courtesy Bob Thomas
179	Brown-Harano Photography
180	Brown-Harano Photography

Notes:
1. Cliff Kirk Photography is no longer in business
2. Brown-Harano Photography has changed ownership
3. *Telegraph-Bulletin* is presently *North Platte Telegraph*

Comment:

As noted in my Preface, most of the photos were taken nearly fifty years ago. Despite reasonable attempts to determine the original photographer, there are numerous instances where I could not, whereupon I designated the credits as "unknown."

Made in the USA
Middletown, DE
19 November 2014